CTC graduations are held around the world. Recent Europe graduates are pictured in this photo.

FINDING A WAY

CENTRAL TEXAS COLLEGE

THE FIRST 50 YEARS

BY J. ERIC HAZELL

Dedication

**DURING ITS FIRST FIFTY YEARS, THE
REMARKABLE SUCCESS OF CENTRAL TEXAS
COLLEGE AROSE FROM THE WILLINGNESS
OF MEN AND WOMEN TO WORK ANY HOURS
IN ANY CONDITIONS TO ACCOMPLISH THE
SCHOOL'S EVER MORE AMBITIOUS GOALS.**

**THIS BOOK IS DEDICATED TO THEIR
FAMILIES—ESPECIALLY THE LATE DR. LUIS JAC-
MORTON, PARKER E. MEYER, JOHN K. MORTON,
AND LESLIE G. GREEN.**

The Donning Company Publishers
184 Business Park Drive, Suite 206
Virginia Beach, VA 23462

Lex Cavanah, General Manager
Barbara B. Buchanan, Office Manager
Richard A. Horwege, Senior Editor
Jeremy Glanville, Graphic Designer
Monika Ebertz, Imaging Artist
Kathy Snowden, Project Research Coordinator
Nathan Stufflebean, Marketing and Research Supervisor
Katie Gardner, Marketing Assistant

James H. Railey, Project Director

**THE
DONNING COMPANY
PUBLISHERS**

Library of Congress Cataloging-in-Publication Data

Hazell, J. Eric.
    Finding a way : Central Texas College, the first 50 years / by J. Eric Hazell.
        pages   cm
    ISBN 978-1-57864-936-5 (hard cover : alkaline paper)
1. Central Texas College—History. 2. Community colleges—Texas—Killeen—
History. 3. Educational innovations—Texas—Killeen—History. 4. Distance
education—United States—History. I. Title.
    LD881.K45H28 2015
    378.764'287—dc23
                            2015021558

Printed in the United States of America at Walsworth

Table of
CONTENTS

FOREWORD

Dear Friends,

It is my privilege to serve as chairman of the Central Texas College District Board of Trustees. In that role, I am proud to present this abbreviated history of our college.

I have had the privilege of watching Central Texas College grow from an idea to reality and could not be more proud of the institution we have become. Our commitment to serving our community—which includes our military community—is evidenced by our thriving Texas campuses and our sites on military installations worldwide.

This history focuses on some of the people and events that brought us to where we are today. We began our journey officially in 1965 with approval from our local voters to form a college district to serve our community. From the beginning our focus was to provide tailored, accessible, and quality education for our community regardless of the location or perceived obstacles.

Our faculty, staff, and administration have a fifty-year legacy of creating something from nothing and turning skeptics into believers. The determination and support of community leaders and citizens was the key to the birth of our college and to its continuing success.

Sincerely,

Mari M. Meyer

PREFACE AND ACKNOWLEDGMENTS

This book tells the story of the creation and evolution of Central Texas College and its impact on those connected with it. Rather than a comprehensive account, it is both a broad overview and a type of micro history, the latter focusing on specific elements that illustrate the defining characteristics of CTC as a whole. Other programs and people not discussed exemplify those characteristics just as effectively but have been omitted primarily because of limitations of space.

Space dictated other omissions. An example is the way CTC contributes to economic development in the region. The American Technological University provided trained personnel for Ross Perot's Electronic Data Systems, and those personnel also helped establish the processing system for what is now the First National Bank of Texas. In addition, CTC helped bring Sallie Mae to Killeen, and it also provided the land for Metroplex Hospital. Such contributions merit at least a brief mention.

The source material includes oral history interviews, primary documents, and secondary sources. As personal commentary mediated through memory, interviews are highly subjective. I have confirmed information from interviews with other documents when possible. Also, as an informal work, this does not include in-text citations or footnotes. The Bibliography lists all sources.

This book is part of an anniversary celebration. However, despite its emphasis on the celebratory, I find the positive assessments of Central Texas College remarkable. When you turn on a recorder and ask people for their opinion, they tend to give it, whether positive or negative. And while I did hear criticism, the administration, faculty, retirees, and community members spoke, overwhelmingly, in glowing terms about CTC.

In short, as a professional historian with considerable experience writing institutional history, I maintain that this represents an accurate overview of the college's history and culture.

Thanks first to Barbara Merlo. Thanks also to Brian Sunshine, Deba Swan, and the very helpful staff at the Hobby Memorial Library. Thanks to those who reviewed sections: Mary Kliewer, James Nixon, Max Rudolph, Joan Waldrop, and Kenneth Walker. Thanks to Suzi Chapman and Terry Hazell for reviewing the entire manuscript, and especially to Jim Yeonopolus, whose comments substantially improved the coherence of the book as a whole. Any mistakes are mine.

CENTRAL TEXAS COLLEGE®

CHAPTER ONE

FROM VISION TO REALITY:
CTC'S ESTABLISHMENT

President Lyndon B. Johnson was the featured speaker during the Central Texas College grand opening ceremony.

"This dedication tells us something important about the real purpose of democracy. That purpose is fulfillment for every individual."

—PRESIDENT LYNDON JOHNSON AT THE DEDICATION OF CENTRAL TEXAS COLLEGE

These words, spoken on December 12, 1967, in front of more than twenty thousand people, came at the culmination of four years of creative thinking and hard work from men and women dedicated to expanding educational opportunity in Central Texas. Their work was part of a larger trend during the 1960s, a decade in which community colleges were established at the rate of about one a week. Certainly, the president of the United States did not dedicate many of them personally—even those in his home state.

President Johnson's presence, along with an opening enrollment spectacularly higher than predicted, both indicate something about the vision and ability of those who joined together to establish Central Texas College.

Oveta Culp Hobby applauds as President Lyndon Johnson shakes hands with college officials and local dignitaries during the Central Texas College grand opening ceremony.

OBTAINING APPROVAL FOR A COLLEGE

From its conception, CTC's creation required resourceful thinking from people who knew how to spin obstacles into opportunities. In early 1963, Dr. Norman Hall, principal of Nolan Junior High School, and Dan Manfull, executive vice president of the Greater Killeen Chamber of Commerce, met to talk about opening a junior college in Killeen. They already faced a problem that could have ended the idea right there, in that Killeen did not graduate enough high schoolers to justify building a college.

The two men devised a solution that, while potentially feasible, would also cause tougher coordination issues requiring considerable finesse: merge Killeen, Nolanville, and Copperas Cove into one college district. Community colleges typically formed from combining two school districts, but many people thought it impractical to combine three.

Nonetheless, in March of 1963, the Killeen Chamber established a Junior College Steering Committee to examine a possible merger. This included Dr. Hall as chair, Dr. Wallace Bay as vice chair, Burns DuBose as secretary, and Dr. Sidney Young, John C. Odom, W. A. Scott, and Andy Resner, all from Killeen. To provide some balance in representation, Ed Rhode of Copperas Cove and Birt Wilkerson of Nolanville also served.

> The University of Texas feasibility study predicted an initial enrollment of 125. The same year, *Time* magazine predicted that online shopping would never become popular. Both predictions proved about equally accurate—or more precisely, spectacularly inaccurate— in their underestimations.

Five months later, the Chamber allocated $500 for a professional feasibility study. The Kellogg Group and Dr. C. C. Colvert, professor at the University of Texas and consultant in junior college education, conducted the study in 1963–64.

What occurred next set a precedent that seemed to plant itself in the original genetic makeup of the college, becoming a trait it displayed repeatedly: converting skeptics to believers. In April 1965, mayors, city managers, school superintendents, representatives from Fort Hood, and many citizens met a survey team from the State Board of Education for a round of briefings. However, like many officials across the state, these visitors doubted that the region could support a college.

At the end of the day, the survey team recommended that the State Board grant permission to hold an election.

That was the first tangible success. And, as with any such event, the accomplishment depended less on the day of presentations than on the months of preparation. The survey day required considerable coordination—from not only three school districts but also two counties. That meant a lot of correspondence, conversations, and presentations at civic clubs and other organizations. The process could have stalled at many points along the way, but by the time the survey team visited, the Steering Committee had won the necessary endorsements.

The Bell and Coryell County Commissioners' Courts likewise approved the formation of a college district, and a temporary six-member board formed with representatives from each town.

Cleo Bay, president of the Greater Killeen Chamber of Commerce at the time, ran Modern Foods, a major grocery store in the city, and he eventually served on CTC's Board of Trustees. In his later years, when asked about his most important accomplishment as president of the Chamber, he replied that without question, it was the appointment of this interim board in preparation for opening Central Texas College.

In the general election on July 10, 1965, residents of the three towns voted their approval by a 9 to 1 margin, demonstrating the overwhelming community support for the new Central Texas Union Junior College District. The first Board of Trustees was elected, the name Central Texas College was chosen, and in October 1965, voters approved a $2-million bond issue.

The University of Texas feasibility study predicted an initial enrollment of 125.

The same year, *Time* magazine predicted that online shopping would never become popular.

Both predictions proved about equally accurate—or more precisely, spectacularly inaccurate—in their underestimations.

Killeen Area Junior College Vote Scheduled For July 10

BELTON — An election has been set for July 10 to create a junior college district comprising the Killeen, Nolanville and Copperas Cove school districts and for the election of a board of trustees.

Bell County Commissioners called the election at Monday's meeting following the presentation of a petition signed by 111 persons in the county affected by the proposed district.

Wallace Bay and Bill Bigham presented the petition after presenting a similar petition to the Coryell County commissioners Monday morning.

The Coryell court also set July 10 as the date of the election, contingent on the action by the Bell County court.

Details of the election must be worked out by an interim board of trustees and the cost of the election must be borne by the interim board.

Bay said that there would be about 4,100 eligible voters within the proposed district.

There will be two issues on the ballot for the July 10 election. One proposition will be to create the junior college district and the second will be to elect a permanent board of trustees.

If the district is created and a board elected then plans can be formulated for the junior college plant and its financing.

The district will be responsible for the land, buildings and equipment and a later election will be called to levy a tax to finance the college.

Estimated cost of the junior college is $1,175,000 for the first year, which includes land, buildings and equipment.

With a student load of 450 students, 60 per cent of the operational cost of the school would be provided by the state, 23 per cent from taxes and 17 per cent from tuitions, Bay said.

The estimated tax which will be needed is 22 cents per $100 valuation.

The predicted enrollment of the proposed college is 155 students the first year and a steady increase to 525 students by 1970.

The Texas Board of Education approved a junior college for the Killeen area in April.

Members of the interim board are Bay, Dr. W. A. Roach and Bigham, all of Killeen; Birt Wilkerson of Nolanville; J. A. Dossett, Marvin Mickan and Mrs. L. D. Frederick, all of Copperas Cove.

All members of the interim board have indicated that they will be candidates for the permanent board.

Local newspapers alert the public about the scheduled date to vote for a local community college in central Texas.

LOCATION AND LEADERSHIP

Seeking a site for the new college, CTC Board members spoke with Lieutenant General Ralph Haines (Commanding General, III Corps and Fort Hood), who, to CTC's great fortune, had dedicated his career to improving education for soldiers. At the time, General Haines chaired the board in charge of restructuring Army officer schooling, and a few years later he would set up the Noncommissioned Officer Education System (NCOES). In 1965, he helped the college district acquire, from Fort Hood at no cost, 103 acres straddling Bell and Coryell Counties. A provision transferred ownership of the land to CTC after twenty years.

General Haines later recalled this work. First, he helped assure Coryell County officials that they would be full partners in the project, "by drawing a hundred-acre rectangle on my Fort Hood map, whose diagonal was the Bell-Coryell County line." He convinced the military that excessing its land was in the post's best interest. And he later worked with the school on its course offerings, emphasizing the need for evening classes and for coordination with his education center.

CTC and Fort Hood officials survey the land donated by the Army on which to build Central Texas College.

In addition to free land, CTC got virtually free buildings. John Guemple, an assistant commissioner for vocational and technical education with Texas Education Agency, helped the college write grant proposals to offers existing under the Manpower Development and Training Act. Under this act, construction funds could be allocated to community colleges, and CTC was one of the first to take advantage. Five buildings were completed for the first academic year and another four by the second, all for negligible costs.

The very first Board of Trustees for Central Texas College.
Seated, left to right: Marvin Mickan; Guinn Fergus; Mrs.
Linus Frederick, secretary; and J. A. Darossett.
Standing, left to right: Birt F. Wilkerson, vice president; Mr. William Bigham, president; Dr. Luis Morton, chancellor; and Dr. W. A. Roach, treasurer.

Through such strategic planning and skillful maneuvering, an entire community college was built for $2 million.

Most people consider the first college president largely responsible for that financial miracle.

The Board began the search for a president at its initial meeting in July 1965. After sifting through many possible candidates, they narrowed the choices to four. Members visited the hometowns of these men, talking not only to them and their families but also to their

> Any time I had a good idea and mentioned it to Luis, he could make it work. And he would always slap his knee and say, 'I'm glad I thought of that.'
>
> —MARI MEYER

business associates, friends, and other members of their communities. In fact, one Board member later recalled snooping through a bathroom medicine cabinet. His chuckle while recounting the story left it unclear as to whether he was just emphasizing the Board's thoroughness or actually telling the truth.

Forty-year-old Louis Morton, at that time dean of Odessa College, was born in Laredo and received his bachelor's and master's degrees from the University of Houston and his doctorate in history from the University of Texas in 1956. He taught at both his alma maters.

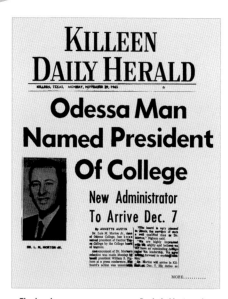

KILLEEN DAILY HERALD

Odessa Man Named President Of College

New Administrator To Arrive Dec. 7

The local newspaper announces Dr. Luis Morton, Jr., was named the first president of Central Texas College.

Bill Bigham of Killeen was the chair of the first CTC Board of Trustees.

When CTC called to tell him a number of knowledgeable people had recommended him for the presidency, Dr. Morton replied that he was happy at Odessa. Board member Bill Bigham responded, "Good, because we are not looking for unhappy people."

Soon enough, Dr. Morton, his wife Mari, and their children packed their bags for Killeen, and he took office on January 2, 1966. This began Mari's nearly fifty-year (and counting) association with the college.

A few months later he posed for a photograph, standing on the ground chosen for the college and holding a set of blueprints. Charles Baggett, who later served on the Board of Trustees for more than sixteen years, recalled that time. "This place," he said, "was nothing but a rocky hill." In fact, "this place" was the same ground about which President Johnson would say, at the college's dedication, "My grandfather drove his longhorns across this prairie on his way to Abilene." In less than two years, the barren hill would be a college opened for business.

A blueprint is a design for translating vision into reality. Blueprint is an apt metaphor for Morton himself, as virtually every colleague of his uses the same word to describe him: visionary.

For example, Bill Bigham recalled that Dr. Morton "had vision way out here that people couldn't comprehend, and he knew how to make it work. There was no limit to his foresight."

Bigham's daughter and former Board member Mary Kliewer likewise states that Dr. Morton "was an amazing hire. He had great vision and knew how to work with elected officials to bring in contracts and to support the military."

Dr. Luis Morton surveys the land and blueprints of what would become the campus of Central Texas College.

The Mortons' four children, three of whom are pictured, grew up watching the birth and infancy of Central Texas College.

Bill Alexander, a CTC student and later dean and deputy chancellor, notes that "Dr. Morton was a magnet for what was happening in higher education and in politics. He knew who to communicate with and he knew how to make things happen."

Joining the chorus, former Board member Bill Roach calls Dr. Morton "probably the smartest visionary I ever knew."

Dr. Morton's welcome statement in the first CTC catalog shows his ideal vividly:

> The standard of quality education along with human understanding and justice as it is known in a free society will prevail at Central Texas College.

> Central Texas College will soon become the respected training and testing grounds for all who wish to enjoy the happiness that comes with struggle and discipline. Surely success will follow as inevitably as the laws of nature are precise for all who come prepared to work and to be helped.

At its core, this vision claims that CTC will become known as an instrument of the American Dream. As we will see, he was right.

Dr. Morton brought with him or soon hired numerous talented people. These included Phillip Swartz, director of fiscal affairs. Mr. Swartz helped oversee the rapid and remarkably cost-effective construction of the facilities. He later became vice president and then briefly chancellor. Kenneth Walker was the first dean, and the administrative staff included Richard Wilson, Earnest Kasprzyk, Sheridan Cavitt, John Moffitt, Darrell Raines, and Major General Edward Farrand. In addition, Tat Lane, Dr. Morton's assistant and the wife of a retired colonel, mentored the new president in military protocol.

Initial CTC staff were housed in an office in downtown Killeen, including Dr. Ken Walker, pictured here on the right.

CLASSES BEGIN

By the summer of 1966, architect Fred Buford from Dallas had completed plans for a library, a student center, and for science, classroom, technology, physical education, administration, and maintenance technology buildings. Dormitories and other facilities waited in the works, and officials stuck their ceremonial shovels in the ground in June.

Mary Kliewer recalls that when she was a little girl, "We would take Sunday drives out to the site of the campus and watch the buildings going up," and she remembers the excitement around the dinner table as her family talked about the latest developments related to the school.

Six universities soon agreed to accept CTC credits, including Baylor, UT, A&M, and Houston. The new school became a member of both the Texas and the American Associations of Junior Colleges. In July 1967, CTC began offering basic academic programs on Fort Hood, and after only fifteen months of construction, five buildings opened in September for the first semester on campus.

Today, Central Texas College's mission statement focuses on affordable, accessible education; clearly this mission existed from the beginning. By the second academic year, the college had opened the Roy J. Smith Student Center, named after the president of Killeen's First National Bank. Smith would prove instrumental in the college's growth. This student center, along with the modern library and well-appointed dorms,

A new era of higher education begins in central Texas as members of the Central Texas College Board of Trustees break ground at the site of the new community college campus.

Construction continues along the walkway between the campus library and Academic Building 104.

Dr. Luis Morton and his sons tour the classroom construction site on the campus of Central Texas College.

wowed both current and prospective students. Also, the college offered courses on Fort Hood for Vietnam veterans and received its initial Southern Association of Colleges and Schools Commission on Colleges (SACSCOC) accreditation. Tuition ran $67 per fifteen credit hours for in-district students, or about $475 in today's money. Lab, P.E., and other fees totaled $15.

Although humorous by today's standards, the first course catalogue shows that students were expected to dress for success as well:

> In general, appropriate dress for women is considered to be suits, dresses or skirts of appropriate length, and sweaters or blouses; for men, full-length trousers, shirts, and sweaters or jackets. Proper shoes and socks or stockings are included in appropriate dress. Personal hygiene and grooming must conform to standards of cleanliness and neatness acceptable in polite society. Beards and uncommonly long hair are not permitted.

Classes offered included Letter Writing, Shakespeare, Dress Design and Dressmaker Tailoring, and the History of England. The catalogue listed more than three hundred classes in all, in addition to those in the Adult Education Program. Students could earn associate degrees in Arts, Science, and Applied Science, and numerous vocational-technical Certificates of Completion.

Dr. Morton worked with Ted C. Connell, an aide to Lyndon Johnson and a former Killeen mayor, to bring President Johnson to the official opening on December 12, 1967. That same day the college dedicated the Oveta Culp Hobby Library, named after the Killeen native, publisher of the Houston Post, and first Secretary of Health, Education, and Welfare. Johnson addressed more than twenty thousand people.

President Johnson arrives with his entourage for the college dedication.

New students accounted for some 2,083 of those in the crowd. Experts had predicted an initial enrollment of 125—just like the experts at *Time* magazine predicted that online shopping would never catch on.

Students line up outside the campus gymnasium (Building 103) to register for the very first semester of classes at Central Texas College.

Ken Word was one of those new students. Years later he would chair CTC's Math Department, and he remembers that first day, when the line of enrollees stretched past the front door of the main building, all the way down to the street where the Bell Tower now stands.

The press, including the national media, called it a Cinderella story. While a common metaphor to depict an unexpected success, in this case it lacks accuracy, because Cinderella is a long-suffering girl who gets rescued.

A better metaphor for CTC might be the Horatio Alger story, in which talent, grit, imagination, and hard work lead one from humble beginnings to a chance at the American Dream.

CHAPTER TWO

FROM OUTPOST TO INSTALLATION:
FORT GATES TO FORT HOOD

> *"The history of the region that became home to Central Texas College is a colorful one, some of it straight out of a Wild West production."*

BELL AND CORYELL COUNTIES

Shortly after the Civil War, Bell County resident Caroline Griffin sat atop a coffin, vowing to marry the man who killed the man who killed her husband. One Sam Hasley considered her worth the risk and carried out the vendetta. Caroline followed through on her word.

The history of the region that became home to Central Texas College is a colorful one, some of it straight out of a Wild West production. Admittedly extreme, Caroline's exploit nevertheless shows that the early settlers brought with them one trait they passed on to their descendants: an ability to get things done.

Western Bell County and southeastern Coryell County are primarily Grand Prairie land. Its rolling uplands, steep bluffs, plateaus, streams, and valleys provided good cover for the natives who lived in the area and fine land for the ranchers who came later.

Philip Nolan, a nineteenth-century soldier of fortune and the man for whom Nolanville is named, was one of the first U.S. citizens in the area. He hunted horses and may have carried out a secret mission to scout the territory for President Jefferson. In 1801, however, somewhere between present-day Killeen and Belton, Spanish soldiers suspicious of his activities killed him.

◄ The Blackburn home, built near Palo Alto around 1863 on what is now the Fort Hood reservation. The cabin was moved in 1954 when the post was expanded and moved again in 1976 to the Killeen Community Center as a historical artifact.
Photo Credit: Historic Killeen, published by the Greater Killeen Chamber of Commerce.

As the white population increased in the middle 1800s, so did tales of outlaw gold, buried treasure, and lost mines. Six Bigham brothers—ancestors of CTC's first Board president—came from Tennessee just before the Civil War, and Oliver Bigham won the contract, at $2,500, to build the county's first jail. Settlers had to be tough: the region's first preacher would walk into the cabin hosting that morning's services, set his shotgun against the wall and his pistol on the table, and commence preaching.

The population of the country grew when one of main feeder routes to the Chisolm Trail ran through Salado, Prairie Dell, and Belton. Ranching and farming opportunities increased, and then in 1881 and 1882, new railroads chugged through Temple, Belton, and Copperas Cove. The region offered key points for shipping cotton, wool, and cattle.

The inhabitants tailored arrangements to suit their ambitions. For example, the Belton Women's Commonwealth got out from under the rule of their hard drinking, unscrupulous husbands by founding a religious commune that practiced celibacy and religious perfectionism. Starting with an egg and dairy business, they eventually bought three farms and managed holdings valued at $50,000. Their founder, Martha McWhirter, was the first woman on Belton Board of Trade.

The counties seemed to attract people who could get things done.

Cotton and other agriculture sustained early Bell County residents. Photo Credit: *Historic Killeen*, published by the Greater Killeen Chamber of Commerce.

FORT HOOD

Few people got things done better than Frank Mayborn, a man instrumental in bringing what became the largest stimulus to growth in the area: Fort Hood.

Mayborn ran the *Temple Daily Telegram* and KTEM Radio Station, and during the Great Depression he helped bring New Deal work programs to the region. He convinced businesses to locate in Bell County, and he teamed with railroad companies and Killeen native Oveta Culp Hobby on many economic development projects.

Through these activities he created key connections in Washington, D.C., and in 1942, his tireless activity helped convince the Army to establish Camp Hood, a Tank Destroyer and Technical Firing Center built on 109,000 acres in western Bell and southeastern Coryell Counties.

In 1943, some additional fifty-one thousand acres were purchased for Fort Hood, and that same year, almost 95,000 troops were stationed there. These included 331 enlisted women from the 159th Unit of the Women's Army Auxiliary Corps, or WAACs, under the command of Colonel Oveta Culp Hobby.

The postwar drawdown left only 11,000 soldiers stationed at the post, but Mayborn remained undaunted. He turned his lobbying efforts to making Camp Hood permanent. Again he succeeded. It certainly helped that the Army post and the town of Killeen formed a cooperative relationship almost from the beginning; in 1952 the two school districts consolidated. And in 1954, III Corps—famous for cutting off the Germans' left flank and liberating Bastogne during the Battle of the Bulge—moved from California to Fort Hood. Now, with a permanent post nearby, the population of Copperas Cove also mushroomed.

A giant American Flag was unfurled on September 18, 1942, marking the opening of Camp Hood. In 1950, Camp Hood was declared a permanent post and renamed Fort Hood. Photo Credit: *Historic Killeen*, published by the Greater Killeen Chamber of Commerce.

The military presence accelerated a longstanding and striking characteristic of the region, and a trait that would continue with Central Texas College: a broad diversity in population. Even before Christopher Columbus, no single native group dominated the area, which was home to the Alabama, Apache, Caddo, Comanche, Kickapoo, Kiowa, and other tribes. In fact, archeologists estimate that some nine hundred different Indian settlements existed in the region.

Camp Hood served as a training ground for soldiers headed to World War II.
Photo Credit: *Historic Killeen*, published by the Greater Killeen Chamber of Commerce.

Before Fort Hood, today among the largest military installations in the nation, there was Fort Gates, an arid outpost established in 1849 near present-day Gatesville in Coryell County. It included among its two hundred or so soldiers men of American, Irish, German, English, Mexican, Scottish, Italian, and Canadian descent.

This tradition of diversity in both counties continued in the twentieth century. In September 1943 (the middle of World War II) the 761st Tank Battalion arrived at Camp Hood. A primarily African-American force—which later received the Presidential Unit Citation—the battalion facilitated integration in Killeen, so much so that in 1957 the district became one of the first in Texas to integrate without incident.

Integration simply amplified what had already been occurring in the area in the 1950s. Many servicemen brought home Korean wives that decade. Some five to ten thousand Koreans lived in Killeen in the years after the war, and during that same decade, women on post formed British, German, and Japanese wives clubs.

Frank Mayborn played an integral role in Fort Hood gaining permanent status in the 1950s, among many other community initiatives.

TEXAS AND THE GROWTH OF COMMUNITY COLLEGE EDUCATION

CTC's beginnings also meshed with two other broad, long-term occurrences: the state's tradition of community college education and the explosive growth of community colleges in the 1960s.

From their beginnings, community colleges served the purposes of democracy. In the late 1800s, the growth of democracy in America meant the growth of equal opportunity, and education became central to that opportunity. While established universities molded students to fit the requirements of classical curricula, community colleges molded themselves to fit the needs of students, offering, for example, vocational and technical education.

Texas helped lead the growth of community college education in America. In the 1890s, Texas Baptists established some of the country's very first two-year institutions of higher learning. In 1914, Texas became one of the first states to accredit junior colleges—nine years before the SACSCOC did (then called

> The junior college should be the "people's college" and be available to all.
>
> **—WALTER C. EELLS, STANFORD PROFESSOR AND FIRST EXECUTIVE SECRETARY OF THE AMERICAN ASSOCIATION OF JUNIOR COLLEGES**

the Association of Colleges and Secondary Schools of the Southern States). In the 1920s, the Texas Junior College Association was founded, and by the end of the decade almost a third of the nation's community college enrollment was in California and Texas.

After World War II, community colleges offered a practical alternative for those using the GI Bill who either wanted career training or who did not want to move their families to a university town. Texas stayed at the forefront of community college education. For example, Texas, Florida, New York, and California led the nation in granting associate's degrees for nursing. Overall, in 1956 Texas had the second highest community college enrollment in the country, at thirty-five thousand.

During the 1960s, community colleges in America proliferated. In December 1963, President Johnson approved the Higher Education Facilities Act (PL88-204), which offered federal grants and loans for twenty-five to thirty community colleges per year. From 1910 to 1960, the country averaged fifty to one hundred new community colleges per decade, but in the 1960s that average jumped to fifty per year.

Community colleges expanded in other ways as well. San Bernardino Valley College in California ran its own TV station, and a few others offered something resembling distance education. As we will see, Central Texas College stayed on the cutting edge of these and many other innovations.

President Lyndon Johnson signs the Higher Education Act of 1965 into law at his alma mater (Southwest Texas State University) now known as Texas State University.

Those who brought Fort Hood and Central Texas College to the region inherited not only this skill for getting things done, but also an appreciation of diversity and a tradition of innovative education that helped provide the equal opportunity at the heart of American principles.

CHAPTER THREE

FROM COMMUNITY COLLEGE TO EDUCATIONAL COMPLEX:
THE FIRST TWENTY YEARS

When Lyndon Baines Johnson honored us by dedicating Central Texas College, he did so to the service "of all the people." By this he meant that it was the sacred duty of everyone associated with this institution to do everything in their power to help as many people as possible, to the end that they too might share in the happiness which comes with achievement and success.

With these moving words, Dr. Luis Morton began the academic catalogue for the 1969–1970 school year. And in its first two decades, the accomplishments of Central Texas College managed to match his soaring rhetoric. It would seem impossible for the school to continue exceeding expectations to the same extent as it did with its initial enrollment, but that is exactly what happened.

In large part, CTC exceeded expectations—spectacularly—because its people continuously devised and ingeniously implemented new ways of expanding its mission and delivering a high-quality education tailored to the circumstances of its students. This was especially the case with the United States military, first at Fort Hood and then around the globe.

◀ School President Luis Morton, Jr., was called a visionary by many in influencing the role CTC now plays worldwide in meeting the educational needs of the military.

The computer science building was added in 1975 to a growing campus.

PROJECT TRANSITION

More than any other factor, Fort Hood explains the high initial enrollment at CTC. In fact, during the first semester, more than 83 percent of the students were soldiers or family members of soldiers stationed there. The college's work with Project Transition aptly illustrates the way it developed effective methods for working with the military.

Project Transition was a Department of Defense/Department of Labor program started in 1967 to deliver education and job training to soldiers—primarily Vietnam veterans—prior to their discharge. DOD directed implementation at 205 installations across the country, and Fort Hood was one of those.

It is a long way, however, from a directive on high to implementation on the ground. Most installations considered the program simply another bureaucratic intrusion and did little to implement it. In 1968, the Education Center at Fort Hood discontinued the few Project-based courses it offered, because of low participation. At Fort Hood and elsewhere, Project Transition floundered.

In the meantime, CTC became the first junior college with a contract partnership for Project Transition, and responsibility for implementation belonged to Kenneth Walker. Dr. Walker had worked for Dr. Morton at Odessa Community College, leaving in 1965 to become the youngest ever Dean of Students

Fort Hood soldiers enhance their careers and prepare for life after the military through classwork at Central Texas College.

Original CTC administrative staff member Ken Walker.

Phil Swartz, seen here on the right, provides a tour to an Army general in 1968.

at the University of Texas Medical Center in Galveston. Before leaving Odessa, he told Dr. Morton, "someday you are going to be a college president, and I would like to work for you again when that occurs."

He did not wait long. The next year he came to CTC and soon became dean of the college and then vice president.

Walker's primary difficulty derived from the wording of the directive, which stipulated that colleges should remain passive bystanders that respond to requests from the military installation. With interest at Fort Hood low and sinking, the project therefore seemed dead on arrival.

Unwilling to lose the opportunity, CTC traded formal procedures for informal channels. Dean Walker contacted the Texas Education Association (TEA), and they all agreed: the funding for the project would go somewhere, which might as well be Texas, especially considering that it could help provide trained manpower for the state. TEA contacted the Texas Employment Commission (the organization responsible for Transition) and secured its support for working with CTC.

Also, President Morton met several times with the commanding general at Fort Hood, finally persuading him to contact the Education Center on post. Dean Walker worked the same approach with Russell Hantke, the Project Transition officer and liaison with CTC. In April 1968, TEA representatives met with the director of the Education Center and his superior, the deputy assistant chief of staff, about funding and about using CTC's brand-new facilities for classes.

These efforts got it done. In May, the Education Center requested nine courses at CTC as part of Project Transition.

In June 1968, a bus from Fort Hood full of soldiers eager to continue their education rolled onto campus for enrollment. Courses in automotive tune-up, drafting, law enforcement, and others began on the 24th and were taught Monday through Friday. Prospective employers often visited the classrooms, and a year later, the first graduation occurred. In its first three years, the program enrolled 1,624 students. 1,264 completed with certificates—almost 80 percent—and 1,062 passed the exit tests needed to earn college credit.

Overall then, CTC initiated and coordinated discussions among the TEA, the Texas Employment Commission, the Fort Hood commanding officer and his subordinate staff office, the Department of Defense, and the U.S. Department of Health, Education, and Welfare. Dean Walker was invited to a nationwide conference in Washington, D.C., to give a presentation that would provide a model for other institutions. In 1973 Walker completed his doctorate at UT, with a dissertation on CTC and Project Transition.

All this is hardly what one would call acting as a passive "bystander that responds to requests." Rather, it was finding a way to get the job done.

Central Texas College was becoming the benchmark for developments in military education.

Students used the campus computer lab to complete assignments.

THE AMERICAN EDUCATIONAL COMPLEX

CTC's success with Project Transition signaled just one part of the college's metamorphosis into what President Morton called an "instructional organism, partially public and partially free enterprise . . . involved in instruction, research and development, and business services." This "total education concept" meant expansion on both ends of the community college to include, on the one end, a high school, and on the other a research institute and an upper-level university with graduate programs. This growth led to renaming the institution the American Educational Complex, or AEC.

Originally, four organizations made up the complex and operated as part of the Central Texas Educational Corporation: the American Preparatory Institute (API), Central Texas College (CTC), the American Technological University (ATU), and the Research Institute for Advanced Technology (RIAT). The American Technological Institute (ATI) was added later.

People often misunderstood the AEC's administration. Based on programmatic functions, it created an institution for each function: high school (API), occupational (ATI), lower division college (CTC), upper division college (ATU), research and development (RIAT). In turn, "systems" departments supported all the institutions: student services, financial services, facilities management, and so on. The various campuses administered the programs, used systems departments to do so, and also utilized local services at the site level.

President Morton comtemplates the world.

AMERICAN PREPARATORY INSTITUTE

In 1973 CTC officials established the American Preparatory Institute (API), a private high school primarily for soldiers. API provided an innovative, "competency-based" education for the country's all-volunteer Army—an Army in which many had never completed high school.

API arose in part from the success of the college's Compensatory Education Program with Fort Hood. When word of this success reached General Robert Fair, commander of the 2nd Armored Division, he expanded the program so soldiers could earn a full diploma, as opposed to a GED.

A junior college could not operate a high school, but predictably, CTC found a way to get it done and turned skeptics into believers along the way. Texas did allow private, non-profit high schools, and with a little imagination, the Central Texas Educational Corporation could define its articles of incorporation in a way that fit this need. In late 1973, Phillip Swartz, Drs. T. C. and Charlotte Smith (consultants from a nationally renowned education center in Dallas), the director of compensatory education, and Jim Yeonopolus (API's assistant superintendent of student services) visited the TEA to plead their case.

In early 1974, API became the first competency-based high school program in Texas.

"Competency-based" means teaching behaviors necessary to succeed in a career by translating those behaviors into educational objectives. Typically self-paced, it mixes academic content and career preparation. As with any educational innovation, this one confronted doubters. In response, Jim Yeonopolus says: "Seat-based education doesn't necessarily make you smarter. It just means you sat there longer."

API took off like a rocket. Programs started at Fort Hood in September 1974. Thirty-nine diplomas were granted in November, and more than twenty-six thousand students attended over the next four and a half years. The college exported API programs to Fort Leonard Wood and then to Berlin. By January 1977, fifty-three additional sites opened in Germany and some thirty thousand students had received instruction. In 1978, API won a contract for providing functional literacy skills to Pacific

"IF THERE WAS SOMETHING BETTER, CUSTOMERS WOULD GO BUY IT. THERE IS NOTHING BETTER THAN API."
—JIM YEONOPOLUS

Fleet Navy High School Studies Program (NHSSP) Afloat Programs, and in the next two years that spread to Guam, Subic Bay (Philippines), and Yokosuka (Japan). Ten years later, API offered courses at twenty military installations in America.

The success was sustained through many challenges. For example, in 1978 the military simply terminated all high school education programs. A few years later, the Army stopped funding its high school diploma plan as an on-duty program. Undaunted by these and other changes, CTC/API perpetually reinvented itself and remained the largest provider of any pre-college programs, whatever they were called. This included the far-reaching Basic Skills Education Program (BSEP) and Academic Skills, which started in 1979, and by 1982 included Continental United States sites from coast to coast as well as Outside Continental United States sites in Korea, Panama, Guam, and onboard Navy ships.

A dedicated group of curriculum and program specialists managed these reinventions. When API opened in Europe, employees created core sets of printed materials, books, and equipment. A decade later this basic concept had morphed into a competency-based skills program that could be modularized and exported around the globe. The critical component was consistency. API was not a college, and so administration, faculty training, instruction—all of these required uniformity across all sites. Sites provided CTC with information on student needs, the learning environment, and access to resources, and CTC/API staffers designed a program consistent across objectives yet also tailored to specific circumstances.

Military students worldwide enrolled in the American Preparatory Institute to receive a high school diploma.

The product did the same thing with accreditation officials as it did with the TEA—it converted doubters into true believers. Suzi Chapman became API's superintendent in 1980 to guide the accreditation process. Their report cards at the ready, examining teams scrutinized schools in Panama, Korea, and many U.S. locations. They came back astounded that API could provide exemplary programs to military personnel, taught by fully qualified personnel, and applied systematically across the globe, from the DMZ in Korea to Fort Richardson in Alaska.

Bill Roach, president of the Board of Trustees for eight years, recalls travelling with three very skeptical accreditation representatives to a CTC site in the Philippines. The trip completely won them over. One said, "I've seen kids drop out of my local high school because they broke up with their girlfriend or got kicked off the sports team, and it's just wonderful to see that CTC can provide them with a high school education and even enroll them in a college."

Members of the 1982 CTC Board of Trustees. Dr. William Roach is second from the right.

Central Texas College saw the demand for an upper-level campus in the community early on and created American Technological University, which became University of Central Texas, then Tarleton State University–Central Texas, institutions that form the lineage for what is now known as Texas A&M University–Central Texas.

" CENTRAL TEXAS COLLEGE WAS THE CRADLE THAT DELIVERED HIGHER EDUCATION TO THE COMMUNITY AND PAVED THE WAY FOR THE BIRTH OF TEXAS A&M-CENTRAL TEXAS. "
—MARI MEYER

AMERICAN TECHNOLOGICAL UNIVERSITY (ATU)

The American Technological University composed the third element in the "total educational concept" of the American Educational Complex. At a public meeting in Killeen in March 1973, discussions began on expanding higher education beyond the community college. Only six months later, ATU—a private, non-profit undergraduate and graduate university—opened with 260 students enrolled.

> CTC responded to a demand that its own success had created.

ATU students would "be trained for occupational competency in the world of work." And in keeping with leadership's tendency to pursue the highest ambition, its mission was "to service the technological training needs of the nation." As with API's competency-based education, this undertaking likewise represented an innovation way ahead of its time in higher education. Tier 1 universities in Texas have only recently—in this century—aggressively engaged in such endeavors.

Dr. Morton described how ATU responded to a mandate, especially from the military. The need "for technological instruction here grew so rapidly that it soon became apparent" that CTC had "reached the limits of its legal capabilities to serve its constituency." In addition, the "growing demands" for more educational services at Fort Hood and across Europe and Asia "made it mandatory" that CTC "would need a comprehensive association with a technologically oriented institution of higher learning."

In part, CTC responded to a demand that its own success had helped create.

A CTC staff member presents a diploma to a military graduate of American Technological University, the precursor to today's Texas A&M-Central Texas.

Over time, ATU expanded. In addition to providing bachelor's and advanced degrees in technological education, it also served military personnel specifically, and its mission encompassed both technical and research support across a grand range, including business, industry, government, and the military. Its programs then extended to include more traditional liberal arts degrees such as counseling and criminal justice. In 1989, a name change reflected this broader mission, and the school became the University of Central Texas. Enrollment almost doubled over the next ten years.

In 1999, UCT dissolved and transferred its assets to Tarleton State University, and the Killeen site became Tarleton-Central Texas. Finally, in May 2009, it became a stand-alone public university, now known as Texas A&M University–Central Texas and operating as a member of the A&M University System.

> Texas A&M University–Central Texas derived from the DNA of Central Texas College

The region is extremely proud of A&M's presence, and rightly so. Bringing a public, upper-level university to Killeen occurred in a manner eerily similar to that that established CTC. It required the same tenacious, coordinated effort from military officials, community advocates in Coryell and Bell Counties, and local education leaders. This makes it all the more important to remember that in its origin, evolution, and creation, Texas A&M University–Central Texas derived from the DNA of Central Texas College.

RESEARCH INSTITUTE FOR ADVANCED TECHNOLOGY

The Research Institute for Advanced Technology, or RIAT, made up the fourth element of the AEC. A private non-profit, RIAT provided "applications-oriented research" to the AEC and to the government, especially in relation to computer applications, telecommunications, and engineering and broadcast services.

As with the other elements of the complex, RIAT's scope included local, state, federal, and international entities, and it became the "economic development" element of the college district. RIAT performed telecommunications and computer services for Bell County and supported numerous special projects. It operated the Knowledge Network of Central Texas (KNCT), the college's radio and television station supported by the Corporation for Public Broadcasting. RIAT also formed the basis of the American Group, used in contracting with government entities.

AMERICAN TECHNICAL INSTITUTE (ATI)

In 1981, the district added another institution to the AEC. The American Technical Institute offered certificate programs on the Central Campus and military programs worldwide that were not high school or CTC courses. ATI's competency-based, self-paced curriculum awarded certificates in nine vo-tech departments. Each department included an advisory board of community specialists who ensured currency. In addition, military subject matter experts helped write curricula that met the needs for Military Occupational Specialty (MOS) training. And finally, ATI established a procedure for articulating vocational courses to apply toward an associate degree.

Mary Kliewer, director of human resources, changed hats to become ATI's academic dean, and, along with Ben Wickersham, lead the accreditation process. Eager to travel the world, many people, including presidents of vo-tech schools, lined up to become part of the SACSCOC team. And in December 1985, ATI received its accreditation. As was usually the case with the AEC, the accreditation team came away impressed, with no major recommendations.

ATI often had the highest enrollment of any entity in the AEC, including 54,148 (worldwide) in the 1987–88 academic year. Overall, its graduates excelled—in a small data sample, they scored about fifteen points higher on competency exams than the state/national average.

ATI represents yet another example of CTC's winning financial formula. By utilizing both vocational and military funding in one organization, the school paid for its operations through contracts rather than taxes. Many Bell and Coryell County residents mistakenly believe that their taxes pay for CTC programs overseas, but in fact, contracts provide the funding for education beyond the local level.

Automotive repair was one of many vocational skills courses offered at CTC.

Vocational skills such as automotive repair enable soldiers to learn a second skill once they transition out of the service.

Many students saw the wave of the future and enrolled in computer science classes.

A computer science student (right) discusses the textbook material with his professor.

Students gather to hear a presentation from the CTC administration.

As the AEC developed, the original Central Texas College continued to thrive. Although in many respects a traditional community college, the school combined several characteristics to produce a particularly high quality of education. For one, by the mid-1970s, many faculty members, like those in community colleges across the country, had just reached their early prime. Further, many people moved fluidly through the complex, teaching for API, ATU, and CTC, sometimes not only in Killeen but around the United States and overseas. The flexibility required to teach different types of students—especially the mobile military population—at different levels in different settings facilitated a continuous effort to insure effectiveness and relevance.

Many other efforts unique to Central Texas College helped insure an accessible, customized, quality education. For example, Central Campus departments distributed master syllabi and textbooks to far-flung sites in order to provide some standardization. The effort required considerable coordination and old-fashioned legwork. And yet again, consistent with what had become one of its most ingrained character traits, in the process the school impressed SACSCOC representatives. Dr. David Yeilding remembers that one team, led by the president of Northern Virginia Community College, "asked some tough questions, but the administrative machinery of the distribution of syllabi and textbooks really impressed them."

In sum, in its first decade, the uniqueness and proliferation of the AEC engendered among education officials a skepticism that was repeatedly dissolved as they witnessed the superb quality of customized instruction each institution offered around the globe.

AN AGE OF EXPANSION

Overall, CTC/AEC experienced almost dizzying growth in its first two decades:

- In 1970, Lieutenant General Beverly Powell, Commander of III Corps and Fort Hood, helped convey an additional 441 acres to the college. Fort Hood, he noted, was "the only military installation in the United States that has a college on the reservation."

- In December 1970, former President Johnson and Lady Bird visited Central Campus again, this time to dedicate his presidential memorial and the Lady Bird Johnson Center for the Performing Arts.

> By 1975, CTC offered to the military more training and education through Tuition Assistance than any other college or university.

- In 1972, CTC took Project Transition to Germany, a major breakthrough that helped the college expand throughout Europe. The Nursing and Aviation Technology Buildings were completed. CTC became the largest provider of voluntary education and training programs for the Army in the continental United States.

- By 1973, CTC had been designated a Servicemen's Opportunity College (SOC). Credits that military students earned during relocations would transfer to CTC, and credits they earned from CTC would transfer to other SOCs.

- In 1974, the college began offering associate degree programs in Scotland and Italy for the U.S. Navy Shore Program, and academic programs and vocational training for the entire U.S. Army in Europe. The same year, the Farm and Ranch Management Building opened at the Killeen campus.

- By 1975, CTC offered to the military more training and education through Tuition Assistance than any other college or university in the United States. Courses were offered at seventy-five sites. Also, the first Continental Campus opened, at Fort Leonard Wood, Missouri.

A growing number of soldiers were taking automotive repair courses at CTC in 1975 as CTC added contracts in Europe and the Far East and was provided classroom space at military installations like Fort Leonard Wood, Missouri.

- By the end of the 1970s, CTC taught at more than 150 sites, including Alaska, Fort Lee (Virginia), the United Kingdom, Belgium, Spain, Turkey, Korea, and Navy College Program for Afloat College Education (NCPACE).

- By the early 1980s, CTC had locations in fifteen states, Central America, eight European countries, and four countries in the Pacific Far East. New facilities at Fort Riley, Panama, Subic Bay (Philippines), and Yokosuka (Japan) made a total of ten major campuses.

- In 1982, Central Campus opened the fifty-thousand-square-foot, state-of-the-art Sid Weiser Vocational Skills Center. Billy Don Everett, executive director of the Central Texas Manpower Consortium (now Workforce Development) helped win the Department of Labor grant. The Center's Board consisted of the six county judges in Central Texas (Bell, Coryell, Mills, Lampasas, San Saba, and Milam).

- The 1983–85 catalogue noted that the institution would soon "pass the one million mark in students served."

- CTC expanded in other ways during the 1980s as well. To name just one example: In a very tangible expression of its mission to provide accessible education, the college added a Handicapped Student Services Department, ten years before Congress passed the Americans with Disabilities Act.

CTC employees at Camp Yokota Air Base in Japan get in the holiday spirit.

President Johnson returned to Killeen for a second dedication, this time for the Lady Bird Johnson Fine Arts Center.

"EVERYBODY ALWAYS FOUND A WAY"

Administration, faculty, and community advocates who knew how to get the job done and who worked to accomplish it—these created CTC's success. An overarching operational philosophy guided their work: making education accessible on student terms while complying with standards of quality. Run from the beginning as a student-centered institution, CTC has always modified program content, delivery systems, and support services to address student needs. Equally important, the college does this within the framework of quality and accountability.

Some of CTC's student-centered innovations have become so commonplace now that it is difficult to believe people ever considered them problematic—but they certainly did. For one, CTC officials helped formalize the method for state funding of college credit, vocational-technical courses, which were often disparaged in the 1960s. Two other innovations involved what today we call "transparency." First, schedules showed which professor taught which class, a feature many other colleges considered kowtowing. Also, professors were required to print syllabi with weekly schedules, so that students, especially soldiers, would know what they missed during an absence.

> ## We were consumed with the college.
>
> **—MARI MEYER, SPEAKING ABOUT HERSELF AND DR. MORTON, PHIL AND BARBARA SWARTZ, AND KENNETH AND PAULA WALKER, IN CTC'S FIRST YEARS**

Explaining CTC's success starts with the vision from the top. Bill Roach notes that hiring Dr. Morton was "the smartest thing the Board did." Morton "knew we wouldn't be able to raise that much from the tax base" and therefore turned to contracts, primarily with the military but also with government at all levels and with many other entities. Dr. Roach adds, "Most colleges and universities would be better off if they learned how to earn more of their money rather than spending the taxpayers'. We earned our money before we spent it."

Jim Yeonopolus, interim chancellor, says Dr. Morton "didn't want to be held down to the everyday trivia. He was dealing with senators and generals." Dr. Morton frequently lobbied for CTC and represented junior colleges at conferences and political functions. Also, Dr. Roach recalls many dinner parties at the Mortons' house and many dignitaries who attended, including politicians, education officials, and "every General that ever went through Fort Hood." Dr. Morton's wife Mari "never put on any airs and was a very good hostess. They put in a lot of work and effort after hours."

One particularly impressive result of all this activity: contract education enabled a tax on operations and maintenance funds at less than half the rate of the average for Texas junior colleges.

Sid Weiser also managed to get a lot done at dinner. A native of Hamilton who later moved to Lampasas, Mr. Weiser was an executive director of the Texas Department of Community Affairs and later a trustee of Metroplex Hospital and president of the Central Texas College Foundation Board. In 1975, while in Korea visiting his daughter, Mr. Weiser received an invitation for dinner with General Richard Stilwell, Commander of United States Forces, Korea. Sid mentioned bringing API to Korea and the general asked, "How long will it take?" Mr. Weiser flew home and called Dr. Morton at 2:30 in the morning. Three days later Dr. Morton was in Korea, followed one day later by Phil Swartz, and by the end of that day the contract was signed.

> Our ability to get the administration to adjust to the marketplace rapidly has been the key to our successes.
>
> —BILL BEEBE

Ted Connell likewise spurred the college's success, along with the region's generally. Killeen's mayor from 1962 to 1966—during the time CTC was established—Connell became one of Lyndon Johnson's closest advisors and helped bring the president to the dedication ceremony. He also led the establishment of Rio Airlines in 1970, which linked Killeen, Temple, and Waco to Dallas, Houston, San Antonio, and other cities.

Roy J. Smith, another community advocate, also proved instrumental in CTC's growth. A prominent Killeen businessman, Smith served as civilian aide to the secretary of the Army for twenty-five years. Like the Mortons, Mr. Smith hosted numerous dinner parties to chat about matters of importance to the college. Bill Roach notes, "he could open doors in Washington that none of the rest of us could," and adds, "If I went to a Korean post I would meet with the education officer, but if Mr. Smith came, we would meet with the commanding general."

Dr. Roach himself facilitated CTC's expansion. The treasurer on the first Board of Trustees and then its president for eight years, he focused especially on the school's relationship with the military. He remembers travelling in Korea once, performing an auto mechanics inventory in the morning, and presenting a graduation speech that same evening. "I did everything from being a flunky to being an executive."

He boasts, "CTC could put a community college campus anywhere in the world where there was a military base."

Ultimately, however grandiose the missions of the AEC components sounded in concept, they succeeded in practice because of the staff's considerable—sometimes comic—efforts. As Phillip Swartz aptly notes, "Without the people to implement them, visions don't mean anything."

Consider the following:

- At Fort Polk (Louisiana), faculty taught in day rooms rather than education centers, so CTC staff and maintenance men packaged BSEP curriculum sets in a dozen foot lockers, trucked them from Texas to Louisiana, and distributed them across the post.

> There was never a time when anybody said, 'I can't do that.'
> —MARY KLIEWER

- Sharon Davis, currently the director of distance education and educational technology, sat in the bed of a pickup in Korea and delivered API curriculum to dozens of sites. On one particularly adventurous day, her and her driver wandered, lost and out of contact, for seven hours. They found their way back just before—or it may have been just after—everyone started to panic.

- Jan Anderson, dean of the Central and Service Area Campus and former program director for API, got food poisoning the night before a one-day training session in Virginia. The next day, she propped herself up on a desk corner and delivered the material, but only after imploring, "Please don't ask me to move."

- One Thanksgiving, Jan and the site director at Fort Meade shuttled back and forth between post and the Aberdeen Proving Ground, negotiating a contract. At nights, she says, "It was me and the hotel cat."

- Jim Yeonopolus helped set up a group of competency-based modules, requested the construction of a giant box, installed skates on the bottom, and rolled the thing through airports and into Mexico to sell to their government. "Anything we could come up with," he says, "no matter how small or how big, we capitalized on it."

- Once on travel to the Far East, Mr. Yeonopolus encountered an unnerving situation: no site

> **WE BECAME THE BENCHMARK FOR ANYTHING THAT WAS HAPPENING IN MILITARY EDUCATION.**
> —BILL ALEXANDER

administrators, no teachers, and no registration manual—two weeks before classes were to start. He spent his first twelve hours standing behind an archaic copying machine with a registration manual he happened to bring: "You had to lift the lid, put the sheet under, and make one copy at a time. I made twelve copies of that thing."

- Surrounded by people eating dried fish on a train with no air conditioning, Jan Anderson rode to the Hialeah compound in Pusan, Korea. Hot, sweaty, and smelling of fish when she arrived to meet the educational services officer, she opened a can of soda, only to have it spew all over her blouse. Her attempt to clean the stain left simply a soapy, soda-stained shirt. The ESO's office sat at the bottom of a hill, and Jan, assisted by suds and soda, literally slid in to meet him.

- Dr. Johnelle Welsh remembers working for Fred Ostertag in Germany in an office without a door. She helped start the MOS training program and then became director of student services for all Pacific Far East campuses. She stayed there fifteen years, and at its peak, enrollment reached twenty-six thousand. Today, as dean of student services, her office has a door.

- "I need drawings of tractors." This was Jim Yeonopolus' request to the Drafting and Design Department after he discovered that the variety of dialects in Mexico made CTC users' manuals indecipherable in some places. A picture is worth a dozen dialects.

- Joan Waldrop, a former site director at Fort Knox, recalls that Phil Swartz, concerned about information leaks, would FedEx contract bids to her the morning of the due date, leave the final amount blank, and call her to convey the details. She had to ensure that every number across the entire contract added up correctly, and then hand-carry it to procurement, all within a couple hours.

- Trapped in her quarters by a typhoon in Okinawa, API Director Suzi Chapman subsisted for three days on soda, popcorn and Beanie Weenies.

Longtime employees Sharon Davis (front) and Jan Anderson aboard a flight to one of CTC's worldwide locations.

- Bob Criswell, hired as dean of student services, began his first day of work on a Monday morning at 5:00 a.m. and got to go home Tuesday at 5:00 p.m. Mr. Yeonopolus says, "We broke them early."

- In Korea, Bill Roach showed stunned SACSCOC personnel API programs in Army barracks and Quonset huts. He told them, "just because we don't have air conditioning and ivy growing up the walls doesn't mean we don't put out a good product."

Dean Johnelle Welsh makes friends with a snowman at the CTC site in Korea.

These adventures and many others demonstrate the understatement in Suzi Chapman's comment: "Everybody always found a way."

These people who "always found a way" speak with great fondness about the work atmosphere at CTC. Mary Kliewer talks in glowing terms about Woody Shemwell, Bill Alexander, Ben Wickersham, Jim Yeonopolus, Don Mikels, Bob Farrell, Ted Woehl, Johnelle Welsh, Suzi Chapman, and Fred Ostertag. "It was the most dynamic group of peers. . . . we kind of grew up together. Many times you would walk out of the building after working on a proposal, and the sun was coming up. Prospects came fast and we had to work fast."

She adds, "We were given a lot of opportunities." Stated another way, employees, just like students, found their chance for achievement at Central Texas College.

Bill Alexander adds Sheridan Cavett and Robert Criswell to Mary's list of remarkable coworkers. He remembers working night and day for three months in the early 1980s on a contract for the Pacific Command. "The camaraderie and the family relationships that were built during those times of working together to achieve a goal—they were phenomenal."

> **IF SOMEONE TELLS ME, 'YOU CAN'T DO THIS,' OR 'IT CAN'T BE DONE,' THAT REALLY GETS TO ME. I DON'T BELIEVE THAT AT ALL, ABOUT ANYTHING.**
> —JIM YEONOPOLUS

Perhaps better than any other single statement, Mr. Alexander's assessment of Suzi Chapman captures the collegiality and mutual respect among CTC staff during this time: "Suzi Chapman is probably the finest mind you will ever know. If she wants to make it happen, she can make it happen. You will not find another person like her on this earth."

And perhaps better than any other single statement, Mary Kliewer's assessment of the workplace captures these employees' attitude: "It was like working for a major corporation, but our product was education. And the words 'I can't do that' were never spoken."

THE KNOWLEDGE NETWORK OF CENTRAL TEXAS (KNCT)

Long before the term "information age" gained currency, Dr. Morton noted in one of his writings that wealth derives not only from land, industry, and commerce, but also from "the instant retrieval of information." As a result of this insight, and with a $20,000 donation in funds and equipment from Oveta Culp Hobby, KNCT was established. Housed in the Frank Mayborn Telecommunications Center, it began broadcasting on FM 91.3 and Channel 46 in November 1970.

Frank Mayborn (center) is joined by Bill Bigham, chair of the CTC Board of Trustees (left) and US Congressman Bob Pogue (right) during the dedication of the CTC telecommunications building named in his honor.

CTC student Max Rudolph would become the "Voice of CTC" and general manager of the campus public television/radio station KNCT.

Max Rudolph—"the voice of CTC"—came to the college as a telecommunications student in the fall of 1971. He remembers his father out in Hamilton buying an FM radio for the sole purpose of hearing Max talk through it. "This is KNCT FM Killeen," Max intoned throughout his first night on the job, "broadcasting from the beautiful campus of Central Texas College, located in the rolling hills of central Texas midway between Killeen and Copperas Cove." Today Max notes, "That's all I said all night, but he bought an FM radio to hear me."

No anecdote could better illustrate the value CTC brings to the people of Central Texas.

CTC even offered a type of distance learning long before that term became common. In 1975, a $2.2 million Advanced Technology Center was added to the Mayborn Building, its purpose, in part, to house the Texas Telecommuter Grid. Operated by RIAT, the grid offered courses in Austin and Dallas through microwave communications. An instructor taught in Killeen while students in the other locations watched on a television screen. With handsets at their desks, they could ask questions in real time. While technology bypassed this method, the grid nonetheless shows CTC's continuous innovations in offering accessible education.

KNCT steadily expanded. Originally, it operated from 2 p.m. to 10 p.m., Monday through Friday. It became CPB qualified in 1974, which means it started receiving a Community Service Grant from the Corporation for Public Broadcasting. As a result, operating hours expanded to 6 a.m. to midnight, and then eventually to twenty-four hours a day. Through a federal grant in 1975, KNCT-TV started broadcasting in color. It is the fourth oldest TV station in the area, one of the oldest PBS stations in the state, and one of the few licensed to a junior college.

KNCT has also become a highly respected job-training program. Its students have obtained excellent jobs with the Walt Disney Company, the *Washington Post*, and the federal government to name a few.

Mr. Rudolph enjoys telling about an intern placement employee at an Austin television station who simply refused to accept CTC students. Max eventually wore her down, and she agreed to accept one student with the understanding that a single problem would terminate the arrangement. And then, within a few years, she said to Max, "I tell the people at UT after they get their bachelor's degree, do not go to grad school. Go to Central Texas College and get an associate degree. Then you'll really know what's going on."

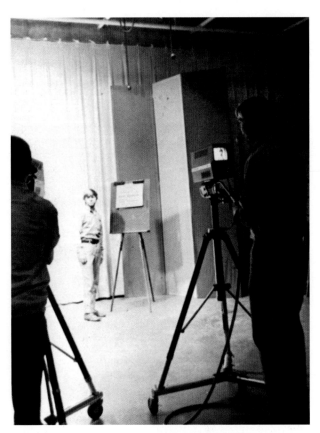

Students get hands-on training in front of and behind the cameras in CTC telecommunications courses.

STUDENT AND COLLEGE LIFE

Just as employees, former students likewise remember CTC's early years fondly. The college completed a dormitory building with boys' and girls' wings for the 1968–69 academic year, and reservations required a $25 deposit. The dorms were always full, dorm parents lived there, and the girls' side locked up at 10 p.m. CTC built a swimming pool in the U-shaped area between the wings. Monica Hull, a former student and now the director of business development for the Copperas Cove Economic Development Corporation, says the most coveted rooms sat on the first floor with a window opening to the pool, because "You may or may not have had a refrigerator in your room that may or may not have had a beverage of your choice in it. And you could just hand it out the window."

Helping to build school spirit were members of the CTC pep squad.

Students enjoyed all kinds of extracurricular activities. The 1970–1971 catalogue listed intramural football, basketball, volleyball, bowling, and table tennis. The 1973–75 catalogue noted some twenty-one campus organizations, including a rodeo club. Ann Farris, Killeen's assistant city manager today, helped start that rodeo club; she participated in barrel racing, bronc riding, and even bull riding. She was good enough to win a rodeo scholarship at Texas A&M. And although telecommunications major Debbie Sublousky did not barrel race for the talent portion of the 1970 competition, she nonetheless won the both the Miss CTC Pageant and the Texas Junior Miss Pageant that year.

The head of the Math Department for many years, Dr. Kenneth Word came to CTC as a student during its first semester. He grew up in Lampasas, and many of his classmates included formal football rivals from Killeen, Copperas Cove, Florence, and Gatesville. They lived in the dorms together and managed to get along, and in fact often continued their athletic exploits. Dr. Word notes that, without a gymnasium but still facing SACSCOC requirements, CTC assembled a universal gym in the power station, right along with all the electrical and mechanical equipment. Students lifted weights on that machine and ran around the school loop to meet physical education requirements. (The following year, CTC built a gym—it is now the Human Resources Building.)

Members of the 1974 Speech and Drama Club promote the semester's production.

The CTC Golden Eagle Tennis Team was a powerhouse, winning the junior college national championship in 1973. In the first year of play, the CTC tennis team placed third in the national junior college tournament.

The school also boasted a championship tennis team. In 1969, their first year of play, the Golden Eagles placed third in the National Junior College tournament in Ocala, Florida. In 1973 they won national championships in both singles and doubles, and they repeated the next year. In 1977 they won first, second, and third place in singles at the national tournament in Scottsdale, Arizona, and also won the national team championship.

The faculty played athletics as well. Student/faculty basketball competitions were waged, and faculty and staff formed softball and flag football teams. Dr. Word remembers playing local teams like Killeen's Blue Moon Café, and he recalls, while rubbing his shoulder, that flag football definitely did not mean noncontact football.

A member of the inaugural class at CTC in 1967 and 1969 graduate, Ken Word would become one of the school's most prolific math teachers, and in 1999 would be named chairperson of the Mathematics Department.

One of the largest student club's was the Central Texas College Rodeo Association. Alumnae Ann Farris (nee Wolfe) is third from the left.

Many employees recall a family-type atmosphere in those early days of the school. English professors John Henderson and Dennis Williams remember Christmas parties with perhaps fifty people present in all, including faculty, staff, and their families. Kids played together, and everyone gathered around the piano to sing holiday songs led by Harry Powers, the director of the physical plant.

Dennis Williams taught English at CTC and remembers a family atmosphere.

Mr. Powers experienced less success in banning coffee pots.

It all started with Gus Rummel, who chaired the Electronics Department for thirty-five years. Mr. Rummel helped establish Texas' first computer repair program, which at one point was named one of the top three in the nation.

He also ran what may have been the state's most successful black market coffee operation. Mr. Powers prohibited individual coffee makers on campus. Undeterred, Gus gutted an oscilloscope (an electrical testing device) and fashioned a fully functional coffee maker on the empty inside. Its front panel intact, the instrument appeared the same as the day it was manufactured. But tiny hinges Mr. Rummel installed at the bottom allowed access to the hidden compartment.

Virtually everyone on campus knew about the contraption except for Mr. Powers. Gus says, "Security people, instructors, a few administrators, and even some of the grounds people who worked for Mr. Powers came by regularly to have a cup."

Mr. Powers also visited sometimes, usually commenting that he smelled coffee. Always one to accommodate, Gus would offer him a cup of the instant coffee they kept on hand, and which, apparently at least, they consumed in large quantities.

The campus in those days reflected its close association with the military. Women on the staff and faculty could not wear slacks, and everyone was required to address each other by last names in front of students or customers. Telecommunications students wore coats and ties when they set up broadcasts for graduation.

Gus Rummel, longtime chair of the Electronics Department, was also known for his coffee contraband.

That was when John Moffett, director of student affairs, kicked Max Rudolph out of school for having long hair. If Max wanted to keep crooning on KNCT about the rolling hills of Central Texas, he had to see a barber. He did.

In the 1971–73 course catalogue, the college removed its description of proper clothes for women students, but it kept for another couple years the prohibition against beards and "uncommonly" long hair for men.

> I was a work study student, and I was able to work in a radio-TV program. The college provided me an opportunity I would have never had.
>
> **—MAX RUDOLPH**

Mr. Moffett and other faculty kept standards stringent in more than just appearance. Trying his best to find an error, Moffett once repeatedly graded a physics test on which Ken Word scored 100. Another time, when Word and a classmate both averaged 93.8 for a class (an A required 94), Mr. Moffett gave them B's rather than round up.

Such occurrences reflected not so much some arbitrary strictness, but rather an insistence that standards remain high. Like John Moffett, Dennis Williams and John Henderson expected the best from their students. When asked about their proudest accomplishments in their forty-year careers as English faculty, both responded that they kept standards high.

At the same time, CTC made students feel wanted and welcomed. As valedictorian of Killeen High, Ann Farris could have attended any state school on a full scholarship, but Richard Wilson, director of student affairs, personally convinced her to attend CTC. And Max Rudolph was an overawed boy from Hamilton adrift in the big city of Killeen, yet Sheridan Cavitt, supervisor of admissions and counseling, personally escorted him around the campus. When Max became chief announcer at KNCT, for $2 an hour, "it was an opportunity to work my way through school, and without it I would have had to drop out. The college provided me an opportunity I would have never had."

> " I'VE DRIVEN THE CTC CAR UP TO NORTH TEXAS AND CHECKED INTO A HOTEL, AND THE PERSON AT THE DESK WAS A FORMER CTC STUDENT. I'VE GONE TO THE 7-11 IN SAN MARCOS IN THE CTC CAR AND FIND THAT SOMEONE INSIDE HAS TAKEN A CLASS HERE. IT'S AMAZING HOW MANY LIVES WE HAVE TOUCHED. "
>
> **—JOHNELLE WELSH**

Similarly, the faculty wives' club *Las Damas* not only promoted friendships and participated in civic activities, but also engaged in outreach efforts on behalf of students. In 1974, for example, dorm girls were invited as special guests to a fashion show in the Lady Bird Johnson Building, and many students modeled for the event.

Then as now, affordability matched academic rigor in importance. In 1975, fifteen credit hours cost $85 for residents (about $365 in today's dollars), $280 for nonresidents (about $1,200 today), and only $500 for European students (some $2,140 today).

Dr. Johnelle Welsh, current dean of student services, started her career as a part-time secretary for the evening college.

Central Campus buzzed with activity. Dr. Johnelle Welsh remembers starting in 1971 as secretary to the Evening College, a major program that ran Monday through Friday. With far fewer educational facilities on Fort Hood then than now, soldiers covered the campus. "You couldn't find a parking space in the evening," she says.

And then there were the armadillo races.

Central Texas College participated in the Association of the United States Army (AUSA), which held an annual convention in Washington, D.C. Every year, groups from all over the country hosted events and sought to present an activity that somehow uniquely represented them.

That was a big deal for a little West Texas kid.

—JOHN HENDERSON, ON SHAKING LBJ'S HAND AT CTC

CTC global presence included sites at military installations across the country and the around the world.

"We decided," Bill Alexander says with considerable satisfaction, "to have armadillo races." The CTC group carried armadillos and an official armadillo race track—of course—to the nation's capital. Word got around, and "everybody and their dog in Washington, D.C., wanted to be at the armadillo races."

Back when he was a student, Bill also escorted Lady Bird Johnson from her helicopter to the ribbon cutting ceremony for the Fine Arts Building that bears her name, and that same day John Henderson shook hands with LBJ. "That," he states, "was a big deal for a little West Texas kid." The student government association even got to attend a VIP event LBJ hosted at his ranch.

Then as now, birds of various sorts alternately pleased and pestered people. In the early 1970s, Dennis Williams remembers, "in that long walkway from the Academic Building to the Library, you had to run the gauntlet of geese."

A much bigger bird perched in the lobby of the Administration Building. There, a golden eagle, blocked off with ropes as in a museum, greeted parents and new students. One year at registration, a young sibling of a new student pointed and said, "Oh mom, look at the buzzard!"

That would have been one frustrated buzzard, because absolutely nothing was dying at CTC. In its first twenty years, the school grew from a small community college across the street from a big military post, to a multinational, total educational complex providing first-rate education from the high school to the postgraduate level. By the mid-1980s it ran six major campuses, had served one and a half million students, enrolled some 250,000 each year, and operated at an annual budget of $64 million. It taught courses at more than two hundred sites in Europe and the Far East, on military bases all over America, and onboard ships for both the Pacific and Atlantic Fleets.

As Bill Alexander says, "Everything about Central Texas College was vibrating."

> Everything about Central Texas College was vibrating.
> **—BILL ALEXANDER**

FOCUS ON

The **Mayborn Science Theater**, opened in August 2003, has thrilled thousands of visitors with its educational and exceedingly entertaining planetarium star shows and laser light shows. Its full-dome, "Immersion Technology" system projects a digital, three-dimensional universe and transports viewers through the Milky Way galaxy.

Dating back to the college's beginnings and reflecting their responsiveness to military students, **Protective Services** programs span the entire range of the criminal justice system. The Police Academy prepares students to pass the peace officer licensing exam, the Department offers Certificates of Completion in Corrections, Law Enforcement, and Fire, and the program overall prepares people for local, state, national, and international agencies.

The **Central Texas College Foundation** supports faculty, staff, and programs at the college and has changed the lives of countless students. Formed in 1992 as a charitable non-profit, the foundation provides about 200 awards through some 170 scholarships annually.

General Robert Shoemaker (Ret.) has been a generous donor to CTC and the community. Here he presents his endowed scholarship, established through the CTC Foundation, to a deserving student, Dante Rose.

PROGRAMS

CTC's **Aviation Department** offers a commercial pilot certificate in a single-engine land airplane, and its courses merge seamlessly with the BS degree in Airway Science at Texas A&M-Central Texas. The school's elite flight team has been the Regional SAFECON champion nine times.

CTC offers a two-year program leading to an associate in applied science degree and the commercial pilot certification with an instrument rating. Students have access to flight simulators to practice and learn navigation before actual plane flights.

One of the flagship organizations at CTC, the **Nursing** program, initiated in 1968, sends graduates to jobs throughout the United States, and many have become nursing professors who serve throughout Texas. Overall, more than three thousand students have graduated from the college with an associate nursing degree. The exam pass rates for the RN, Licensed Vocational/Practical Nurse, and Paramedic graduates all exceed national averages. A new Nursing Center building with a state-of-the-art Simulation Center was opened in January 2011.

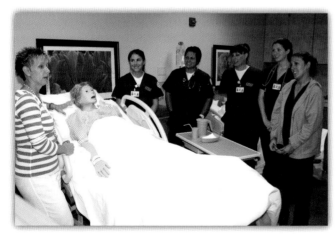 

The CTC Nursing program now includes state-of-the-art technology and equipment including hospital simulation labs, labor and delivery labs, an intensive care unit lab, pediatric care unit, and more. The new nursing facility opened in January 2011.

As a community college, preparing students for important careers like nursing was an early priority for the central campus.

CHAPTER FOUR

FROM VISION TO OPERATION: A NEW ERA

> *When you work in community relations and marketing, you are somewhat separated from the students. But every year at graduation, when the seventy-year-old lady walks across the stage and her whole family stands up with a sign that says 'Way to Go Grandma,' that's when you realize what it is that you do.*
>
> —MONICA HULL

A CHANGE IN LEADERSHIP

Organizational expert Larry Greiner's classic model describes stages through which successful corporations typically progress. In this "Greiner Curve," each stage leads to a transition point—or crisis point—that, if managed well, allows the organization to continue expanding.

According to Greiner, in the initial building stage, growth occurs through a visionary leader's creativity. Expansion then creates a crisis that requires hiring additional specialists. This "growth through direction" stage continues until programs again become too large to manage, which leads to a delegation stage. Here, layers of administrative hierarchy are added and top management focuses less on daily operations and more on overall strategy.

CTC certainly fit the Greiner model. For example, so many people describe Dr. Morton as a visionary that you would think they worked in a cubicle next to Greiner. Likewise, the hiring of Drs. T. C. and Charlotte Smith as consultants for API exemplifies the "growth through direction" phase. Further, Jim Yeonopolus' statement about Dr. Morton perfectly indicates the delegation stage: "He didn't want to be held down to the everyday trivia. He was dealing with senators and generals." And some CTC employees note a tendency in the 1980s for a few top officials to micromanage, another typical characteristic of Greiner's delegation stage.

Dr. Jim Anderson and his wife, Lois, who retired as the dean mmeritus of the Continental Campus.

◀ Dr. Jim Anderson served as CTC chancellor from 1988 to 2011. Under his guidance, CTC established dedicated classroom facilities at Fort Hood in 1989, and later, CTC's administration building which would become the first college-owned building on a military installation. Dr. Anderson was also instrumental in CTC being awarded the first-ever FORSCOM foreign language contract in 2002 and two Worldwide Army Educational Support subcontracts in 2006.

In one of life's baffling ironies, our every character asset contains a defect on its backside. The very traits by which we thrive can, when misapplied, cause harm. In an organization, the visionary who spearheads the skyrocketing success also builds the spaceship on the fly. Proper procedures matter less than reaching the vision.

In careful hands, such an approach can spawn spectacular accomplishments, as with CTC's creative interpretation of policy regarding Project Transition. In other instances, creative interpretation looks a lot like disregard. CTC's extraordinary expansion, along with the web of interconnecting boards and officers of the AEC, eventually created suspicion, which ultimately brought on a management study authored by Terrell Blodgett of the LBJ School of Public Affairs at the University of Texas.

The ensuing investigation and its exhaustive report created the most alarming predicament in the school's history. Each institution in the AEC faced intense scrutiny in regard to its mission, management, and performance. In the worst-case scenario, the school could have shut down, and in fact many believed that is exactly what would happen.

A crisis this extensive could throw a curveball into the Greiner Curve. In that template, after the visionary, a second leader takes charge. This person specializes in planning and operations, cleans up the debris left from building on the fly, reduces careless expenditures, and, perhaps most important, leads a smooth, controlled growth.

Fortunately for CTC, just such a leader had recently arrived. Dr. James Anderson grew up in Pittsburgh, joined the Air Force when he was seventeen, and earned his Ph.D. in economics from Florida State. He taught at the Air Force Academy and the Air University and was appointed a professor of economics. He served a total of thirty-two years, twenty-two as a commissioned officer.

Dr. Anderson's wife Lois worked for CTC as a site director in the Philippines, and when he transferred to the Pentagon, she became the site director at Bolling Air Force Base. When he retired, CTC offered Lois a job in Killeen.

"THE IMPACT THAT CTC HAS HAD ON ME HAS CAUSED ME TO BE THE PERSON THAT I AM TODAY."
—BOBBIE WEAVER, WEAVER AND WILLIAMSON LAW FIRM AND FORMER BOARD MEMBER

Dr. Anderson says that when he found out Killeen had a golf course, he agreed to move. Lois ran CTC's Killeen Mall site, and then the school offered Dr. Anderson a deputy chancellor position. He notes, "And since you can't play golf twenty-four hours a day, I decided I would do that."

In quick succession, Dr. Morton retired, Mr. Swartz became chancellor, he retired, and Dr. Anderson became interim chancellor and then chancellor.

"My furniture," he says, "was still in storage."

Dr. Anderson's leadership style epitomized the coordination phase of the Greiner model. In the initial, "cleanup," step of this stage, the new chancellor faced a full plate. He cut expenses because, as he frankly states, "The first thing was to keep us afloat. It was pretty obvious what needed to be done, but it wasn't easy." He adds that "We had to face reality," and at the same time, "You had to think you were going to succeed."

Fortunately, most of the issues Blodgett raised were solved easily. Dr. Anderson says that during his first meeting with the professor, 90 percent of the items they discussed were "answered and approved before he left."

> Since you can't play golf twenty-four hours a day, I decided I would go ahead and do that.
>
> —DR. JAMES ANDERSON, ON COMING OUT OF RETIREMENT WHEN CTC OFFERED HIM A DEPUTY CHANCELLOR POSITION

CTC cleared those items so easily because it had never stopped offering a remarkable quality of education in remarkably diverse circumstances. Mary Kliewer, who transitioned from ATI to the Board of Trustees during this time, says, "people didn't understand. It was just not like anything else. And when you don't understand and there's a lot of success, things can become suspect. The product delivery was always wonderful."

Professor Blodgett agreed. Many people who know of the report do not know that positive assessments of AEC are scattered throughout. For example, it acknowledges that the accreditation team examining far-flung ATI locations named "very few recommendations or even suggestions for improvement." Further, "representatives in government and other areas" offered "very favorable assessments" of education at AEC. The report also notes that the American Association of Adult and Continuing Education had recently honored Sergeant Alejandro Torres as one of the nation's nine "Outstanding Adult Learners." He earned his high school equivalency from API and his associate degree from CTC.

In tackling other issues Blodgett raised, the new chancellor's efforts clearly fit the operational leadership style Greiner outlined:

- Dr. Anderson started the Faculty Senate to give professors a more direct role in the school's operations. He attended meetings only when invited. In other words, he established the operation and then played his part.

- Dr. Anderson systematized pay raises. "All my life I was in the Service. At CTC, I based pay raises on that. We set up a system. Supervisors could submit a request for an employee raise to a panel, which made a recommendation."

- Dr. Anderson framed a five-year strategic plan. With the help of community leaders—such as Ann Farris, former CTC student and at the time an administrator in the Killeen Independent School District—a process was established to insure input from all participants.

Within a year, the college had turned the corner.

Riley Simpson, president of the Board during this challenging time, said the Blodgett Report "actually strengthened the college and its position with the state officials, because we were cooperative. They learned a lot. Our programs were very different from the typical state community college. We were cutting edge in making our programs available to the community and especially the military around the world."

Similarly, in a comment typical of those about Dr. Anderson, Bill Roach says, "We needed a really sharp person with credibility among college people. Dr. Anderson was just a solid as anyone could be at doing things the right way. He was a person you could put your trust in."

Monica Hull, former CTC student and later its coordinator of public information, says this: "Dr. Anderson continues to be one of the most amazing men I've ever met. He was a great public speaker. Three minutes before he would talk, he would ask me, 'Okay, what am I talking about?' I would say, 'you need to hit these three things,' and he'd just go in and start talking. No speech writing for him. Dr. Anderson was pretty cool."

Dr. Anderson received a commemorative gift from Ronnie Turner and the Welding Department upon his retirement.

Dr. Anderson also cultivated relationships with elected officials, state and national coordinating boards, and the military, and he stayed active in community college associations. Through such efforts, CTC stabilized.

THE ANDERSON ERA

The people of Central Texas College wanted more than just for the institution to steady itself. Across the spectrum, the Board, administration, and faculty wanted to expand. One Board member, expressing the basic consensus, said the school should continue its global contracting services "as long as it provides the same quality of education."

The Board of Trustees and new chancellor guided a remarkable turnaround. Chair of the Board's Finance Committee at the time, Mary Kliewer notes that "we had a lot of flags," and so the Board helped streamline operations by reducing duplication, dissolving RIAT, and consolidating the rest of the AEC back down to its original organization, Central Texas College. Additional restructuring created two assistant deans—academic and vocational—plus three deputy chancellors. These changes in turn lessened suspicion among state education officials and the media. The Board also increased its involvement, meeting more frequently and publishing agenda items in local newspapers. Members more openly expressed dissenting opinions and actively engaged in crucial matters such as delegating contracting authority.

Overall, Dr. Anderson orchestrated a metamorphosis in the college's global mission consistent with his operational style. Jim Yeonopolus, at Central Texas College for most of Dr. Morton's tenure and all of Dr. Anderson's, describes the change with a metaphor: Dr. Morton discovered oil and dug wells everywhere one could possibly dig. The overriding criterion was not production but capability. As a result, many wells produced oil but many did not.

Dr. Anderson changed the criteria. Switching metaphors, Mr. Yeonopolus calls Dr. Anderson a surgeon who cut away the unproductive excess. The criteria for contracting became tougher to meet: Did a service add value to the college and to the community? Could it be effective? And most important, did it bring in more than it cost? Although paramount, the final criterion did not focus solely on money. For example, certain programs added value not always measured in dollars, and in that sense did bring in more than they cost.

Not a native Texan, Chancellor Jim Anderson got here as fast as he could.

In a recent oral history interview, Dr. Anderson says, "We got rid of the undesirable contracts and expanded on the good ones." That sounds straightforward, but it was a painstaking process requiring large-scale, detailed calculations of a great many agreements, and then frequent adaptations afterwards.

THE PRISON EDUCATION PROGRAM

The prison program represents one excellent example of the new leadership in action. Soon after Chancellor Anderson took office, the Gatesville Unit of the Texas Department of Corrections requested college education courses. Under the previous administration, the school would likely have found an effective method of delivering on the request. However, Mr. Yeonopolus, the person charged with the proposal, helped forge a remarkably better contract by working from Dr. Anderson's new framework.

Some of the new criteria were easily met. For example, the connection between education and reduced recidivism meant that a program would clearly benefit the community. On the question of effectiveness though, the idea floundered: could prisoners pass college classes? In order to provide the most useful arrangement, then, Mr. Yeonopolus proposed a full-service educational program, which would include counseling, testing, and placement services, plus job skills training and both remedial and college classes.

Skeptical prison officials balked. However, not having to say yes, just because you can, means you can say no, and when it became clear that CTC would provide this model only, a contract was signed. The program not only thrived but also grew beyond anyone's expectations. It reformed prison education across Texas and was transported to some half a dozen additional states.

Jim Yeonopolus presents a student with her diploma during a graduation ceremony at a prison.

In short, changing administrations did not change the DNA of Central Texas College, which still found a way to convert the skeptics.

Unfortunately, the arrangement later suffered a virtual deathblow when new regulations prevented prisoners from using Pell Grants for education. CTC scaled back, leaving other states but continuing to operate a large program in Gatesville. The Anderson approach still applied—revenue exceeded expense.

Mr. Yeonopolus calls this overall method a "controlled, targeted growth." After terminating the losing contracts, we "ended up with the things we did best. We put all our effort into those. At the same time, Dr. Anderson never stifled our creativity in going after new business. He just controlled the growth by subjecting it to the new criteria."

DISTANCE EDUCATION

Over the next two decades, functioning under this new model of expansion, CTC continued to exhibit its remarkable ability to get things done. Space limitations prohibit a comprehensive discussion of successful initiatives during the Anderson administration, but a few specific examples illustrate the point.

One smashing success has been distance learning (DL), or distance education. The pervasiveness of DL today makes it almost impossible to remember how radical it seemed a short time ago. Questions about academic honesty, student-teacher interaction, technological feasibility, and many others caused considerable resistance among professors and administrators across the country. As a result, establishing distance education at CTC played out with considerable difficulty.

Board members Riley Simpson and Mari Meyer deserve much credit for the impetus, as they both encouraged the college, early on, to participate in what seemed the inevitable future of education delivery. And here it should be noted: from a very young wife hosting dinner

The 1991 CTC Board of Trustees. Riley Simpson and Mari Meyer, who played a key role in the distance education initiative, are seated center and right.

parties in the school's first years, to a Board member helping usher it into the digital age, Mari Meyer has contributed to CTC's success in ways that are both singular and impossible to measure.

Soon thereafter, Bill Beebe in the contracts office and Jim Yeonopolus recommended to Dr. Anderson that Suzi Chapman lead the effort. Ms. Chapman, former API superintendent, had been working on a classified contract that provided crucial funding during the school's crisis. Having led curriculum development with API/BSEP, she seemed the best choice for distance learning.

Suzi Chapman, center, developed a distance education program with little funding and less than universal support. She is pictured here at her retirement farewell with longtime co-workers Jan Anderson and Sharon Davis.

Mr. Beebe says, "That was the logic we used at the time, and it worked." He adds with a smile, "Suzi blamed us on numerous occasions for doing that to her."

As always, CTC would tailor to military needs. Many recruits joined the Army for educational benefits, and when reassignments interrupted their education, they left the service. The high cost of this turnover led to the creation of eArmyU, or electronic Army University, which provided a retention incentive by allowing soldiers to use their educational benefits while deployed.

CTC started at the beginning—creating a website—and then researched both the quality and technical parameters that would enable a viable delivery system. Eventually, Ms. Chapman was assigned a team, but lingering doubts about distance education meant they still worked with sparse resources. Sharon Davis, today's distance education director, ran course development and faculty training, and Diana Castillo, currently the eArmyU institutional liaison, trained online faculty for Continental Campus.

The advent of eArmyU gave soldiers access to education in deployed environments. Pictured here, a CTC Europe staff member assists a student.

Mr. Beebe acknowledges the pressure at the time. "You can't sell it if you don't have it, so the heat was on. Of course, we didn't give Suzi any resources either."

In 2000, the Army put out a request for proposals for eArmyU. Ms. Chapman says, "We knew that it had to happen. Online learning was going to be the wave of the future if you wanted to respond to the educational needs of the military."

> We were the leaders in the Virtual College of Texas thanks to David Yielding and John Frith.
> **—SUZI CHAPMAN**

Chair of the Math Department at the time, Ken Word recalls that in early 2000 he received a directive to provide statistics and college algebra online—starting immediately. Beginning with technology crude by today's standards and learning on the fly, the department began by providing simple Adobe Acrobat files online. But soon, efforts became systematized and advanced.

Experimentation reigned. The department offered blended (not hybrid) courses, where students with a webcam could stream lectures from a computer. Predictably—at least in hindsight—those students never attended class in person. So a new requirement stipulated that they attend one lecture a week. Within the decade, all homework was administered online, and today, Dr. Word considers the shift to online education the department's biggest accomplishment during his tenure as chair.

As is typical in the oral history interviews conducted for this project, the credit for CTC's cutting edge success gets spread around. For example, Suzi Chapman states, "We were the leaders in the Virtual College of Texas [a collaborative of community colleges] thanks to Drs. David Yielding and John Frith." Likewise, she credits Bill Alexander and Diana Castillo with implementing online education at the Continental and International (C&I) Campuses. Mr. Beebe, in turn, notes Mary Carr's contribution to the transition on Central Campus.

In fact, the way people credit others, in itself, indicates the reasons for distance education's success. Dr. Anderson says, "There was a lot of resistance, including from me, but I was wrong. I didn't see all the possibilities. And our online program just got better and better."

In the end, all fingers point to Suzi Chapman—in a good way. Mr. Beebe sums up the general feeling, saying, "She was the godmother of DL at CTC." Ms. Chapman responds, "I feel good about the people who worked with me and who found low-cost solutions that enabled soldiers fighting for us to continue their education."

The first distance education course, in the fall of 1997, had about five hundred enrollments. Today, online enrollment exceeds seventy thousand.

One could argue that distance education succeeded despite Dr. Anderson's opposition. He in fact acknowledges his resistance. However, a less simplistic interpretation is that his overall approach as chancellor helped ensure that a potentially good program could succeed without his direct blessing. In other words, if he was wrong, then the procedures he established, relying as they did on capable people who felt free to voice their disagreement, would correct matters. This is not management; this is leadership. A bigger ego would have ensured failure.

FORT HOOD

The growth of Central Texas College on Fort Hood provides another excellent example of the school's ability to get things done and to tailor quality education to the needs of the students. In late 1980, James Nixon, a retired Army aviator, came to CTC as a part-time curriculum developer, and five years later he became dean of the Fort Hood campus. Stationed there for eight years in the 1970s, he had insight into the problems of educating soldiers with minimal negative impact on mission performance.

His initial situation at Fort Hood evokes memories of Jim Yeonopolus sweating behind an ancient copying machine in the Far East, or Jan Anderson and Sharon Davis perching themselves on the backs of pickup trucks in Korea. Mr. Nixon shared space with the Army Education Center in a barracks and, with no desk, deposited his open briefcase on top of a filing cabinet and worked while standing.

In the mid-1980s, the college program on post consisted primarily of hospitality and criminal justice courses, and it was so small—about three hundred enrollments annually—it was run by the CTC Fort Hood director's secretary. In other words, tremendous opportunities existed.

However, soldiers faced considerable difficulty with the traditional sixteen-week semester. Commanders generally hesitated to commit them to that long a period. Mr. Nixon concluded, "We needed to make a class available when the soldier had time to take advantage of it." After careful study of the relevant guidelines, "I saw that I could reduce a course to eight weeks, meet all the requirements, and offer a more usable product to the soldier."

Fort Hood would schedule primarily in the evenings, and additionally, sequential courses insured soldiers would never have to wait a term for a class offering. The plan created the possibility of completing an associate degree in one year. This five-cycle per year, eight-week course schedule has

since been imitated in various forms
on Central Campus and elsewhere,
becoming just as popular with civilians
as with the military.

Prior to the construction of its current post facility, CTC used temporary buildings for classrooms on Fort Hood.

The program flourished. They quickly
outgrew the classrooms the military had
provided and began leasing space from
Smith Middle School. The arrangement
was effective but expensive, and so, with
the permission of the Fort Hood command and the support of the Army Education Center, the college
built four temporary buildings on a vacant lot. The additional thirty-two courses immediately filled.

Unable to keep pace with the registration, the school received permission to erect three more temporary
buildings, including space for counseling, registration, and student services. By the early 1990s, CTC
Fort Hood enrolled well over a thousand students per eight-week cycle.

The growth continued to accelerate. A corps commander ordered the removal all wooden buildings
on post, which meant destroying both the Education Center and the old Army hospital. The college
proposed that it build permanently on the hospital site, and it offered to include a wing for the ESO
and staff. The building—the first college-owned structure on a military installation in the United
States—was completed in
2001 and housed complete
counseling and registration
services, three computer
labs, classrooms, and all
CTC staff.

The hospitality program
on Fort Hood further
illustrates CTC's success
there. Run by David
Lazarus since 1992, the
classes have always been
extremely popular. In late
2007, when a new food

Soldiers congregate outside the current CTC Fort Hood student services building on post.

The CTC Culinary Arts program on Fort Hood is housed in a former Burger King restaurant, which has been renovated into a fully functional culinary lab.

court opened on post, Dean Nixon sought to add the now-vacated Burger King to the program's facilities. Fortunately, the officials in charge knew Fort Hood's hospitality program quite well, having been the beneficiaries of its expertise at a few dinners. In fact, a Board member, the garrison commander, Dr. Anderson, and Dean Nixon worked out the details of the Burger King agreement during a fish fry. CTC extensively renovated the structure into what is now a state-of-the-art teaching lab.

The hospitality building today, as the former dean notes, "is a prime piece of real estate with a huge sign out front that says Central Texas College."

By 2010, CTC had once more outgrown its space and received permission to build again to support the Army education initiative. It completed a second permanent classroom building (27,264 square feet), and today, under the direction of Dr. Tina Ady, it is one of the very few colleges with its own campus on an Army post. Many CTC students mix and match classes among Central Campus, Fort Hood, and distance education. Enrollments on the Fort Hood average more than ten thousand per year.

Members of the CTC Board of Trustees and Fort Hood officials break ground at the second CTC facility on the post in 2009. The new building opened the following year.

The new classroom building provides another example of CTC's commitment to the military—the college sold land it owned adjacent to the Killeen Airport in order to pay for construction.

Overall, expanding college programs at Fort Hood was a no-brainer, easily matching the "controlled, targeted growth" vision governing the new administration. Like Mr. Yeonopolus, Mr. Nixon places the work in that context: "I discovered that if something made sense, even if it seemed outside the box, the college leadership would buy into it. The more we all did, the more we saw we could do. This is how the Board and Chancellor Anderson were instrumental in whatever success we enjoyed. Also, working with a staff and faculty who could help make it happen made all the difference."

BASIC SKILLS

As with Fort Hood, Continental Campus locations confirm the statement that "Dr. Anderson never stifled our creativity in going after new business." Site directors everywhere, detached as least physically from Central Campus, were allowed to create their own advantages, as long as they worked within the clearly defined new criteria.

Fort Knox offers just one of many examples. In the 1980s, the site offered the Basic Skills Education Program (BSEP) only. Then, administrators created opportunities to teach defensive driving and a test prep course for soldiers. In 1990, CTC began offering two associate degrees, and a little bartering got a room at Fort Knox High School in return for teaching welding there. The college now had its foot in the door for college courses. By 2000, the site added a degree in general studies.

Joan Waldrop, the director at Fort Knox from 1984 to 2008, says, "It was like running a small business." She projected enrollment and expenses and had to function within those parameters. Like all the sites, Fort Knox did its own student evaluations, counseling, financial aid—everything down to cleaning services. Joan says, "We had to be a jack of all trades."

CTC hosts a graduation ceremony for students at Fort Knox, Kentucky.

In addition, CTC's ability to provide accessible education produced tremendous advantages. Another community college offered courses on Fort Knox, but CTC could articulate military experience into college credits. As a result, higher-ranking soldiers could often finish a degree with some ten additional classes. Similarly, a soldier at the other community college could rarely continue classes after a transfer, but one at CTC could enroll all over the world. CTC also formulated a "Two by

Two" program with Louisville, whereby students could take classes at both schools simultaneously and potentially earn a bachelor's degree in three years.

Instructors at the post's renowned Armor School were all ranked sergeant first class or above, which meant high-ranking soldiers populated CTC classes. This, along with the quality of the faculty, leads Ms. Waldrop to note proudly, "Although we were a small site, we had one of the highest percentages for degree completions.

The working relationship with Central Campus further demonstrates how managed growth helped the Continental and International sites thrive.

- Every two years, Dean Lois Anderson brought all continental site directors to Killeen to meet with the financial aid, curriculum, marketing, student services, and other departments. Ms. Waldrop notes, "That support was tremendous. It was much easier to contact someone you already knew. You began to feel a part of the whole."

- Dean Anderson also streamlined management and reduced duplication by funneling directives for Continental Campus sites through her office.

- Similarly, Ms. Waldrop acknowledges the support of Bill Beebe and Maxine Lettman: "If I had a question about anything, from a Department of Labor issue to janitorial help—anything—they would sort that out. Mr. Beebe was terrific."

- When BRAC reductions thinned out Fort Knox, CTC kept enrollments through eArmyU, and in 2008, online enrollments exceeded classroom enrollments.

Every C&I site has contributed its own unique elements to CTC's accomplishments. Each has its own history and culture that merit discussion, but space limitations prevent that level of detail. Fort Knox received the attention it did here because of the way it illustrates the management principles operating at the college.

> " I STARTED TEACHING FOR THE NCPACE PROGRAM IN 2010. I'VE RECEIVED NOTHING BUT KINDNESS AND SUPPORT FROM STAFF, MILITARY PERSONNEL, AND MORE THAN FIVE HUNDRED STUDENTS. WITHOUT THIS PROGRAM, MANY STUDENTS WOULD NOT BE ABLE TO OBTAIN A DEGREE IN A REASONABLE AMOUNT OF TIME OR EVEN AT ALL. IT'S AN EXPERIENCE I'LL NEVER FORGET. "
>
> —VICTORIA BROWN

CENTRAL TEXAS COLLEGE AND TROOP DEPLOYMENTS

On October 12, 2000, when terrorists attacked the USS *Cole*, a Central Texas College instructor was one of those wounded (seventeen died). In the ensuing decade, CTC services in war zones epitomized, as much as at any point in the school's existence, the student-centered, customized, quality education that the college provides and the extraordinary effort its people expend to provide it. In between the chancellors, presidents, and deans on the one hand, and the faculty on the other, a host of test examiners, counselors, college representatives, IT professionals, and other staff toiled away, as they always have, to ensure that everybody—everybody—got what they needed when they needed it.

CTC employees willing to work in such areas signed up for a minimum of six months, received Individual Readiness Training, and lived downrange with the same facilities as our troops in forward operating bases (FOBs). At FOB Salerno in Afghanistan, for example, some half dozen employees served a population of anywhere from two thousand to five thousand.

At one FOB after another, the college delivered education in whatever fashion students could utilize. In traditional courses, soldiers or other personnel with regular schedules met in the Education Center classroom during established days and times. The same distribution network that had for years impressed SACSCOC officials around the world sent textbooks and other materials from Killeen to the European campus to downrange.

CTC Students enjoyed a pick-up game of basketball against students from the University of Maryland–University Campus while stationed in Afghanistan.

Impressive in itself, this schedule composed only a portion of CTC's services, offered virtually around the clock. If a soldier happened by the Education Center at 2:00 in the morning, saw a couple CTC employees still there because of the Internet access, and asked to take a CLEP or AFCT exam, he or she could take that test, right then. The college also served individual units by offering instruction at whatever times soldiers would be at the FOB. Careful record keeping insured they met all requirements. And in at least one instance at Salerno, an instructor travelled blindfolded to a Special Forces compound to teach a criminal justice course.

Students from Fort Stewart, Georgia, are pictured in Iraq in the early 2000s.

Throughout Afghanistan, Iraq, Kuwait, and other areas, Central Texas College personnel operated mini campuses like these. They taught courses, administered tests, recruited instructors, formulated degree plans, and found tents when they couldn't use classrooms. CTC and the University of Maryland University College often organized basketball and flag football games between students from the two schools, with each side designing their own game jerseys. In addition, Mr. Yeonopolus and Dean Gary Kindred traveled to perform graduations in both Iraq and Afghanistan. Overall, any service member or support personnel, with any educated-related question, attending any school, received help from Central Texas College.

CTC Dean Pamela Kennedy served as a CTC field advisor in Afghanistan. Like other deployed personnel, she was required to participate in Individual Readiness Training (IRT) prior to her departure.

Anyone considering academia an "ivory tower" detached from real life would think differently after seeing CTC employees walk five minutes to the nearest restroom, work without air conditioning in the desert, live six to a room, dine for days on frozen pizzas when food trucks were robbed, and shake the dust off every folder of paper, piece of furniture, and article of clothing that they touched.

FOB Salerno certainly earned its nickname—Rocket City. Pamela Kennedy, a counselor at the FOB and today the associate dean of the Fort Hood Campus, eventually considered diving into a bunker during a mortar attack part of a typical day. Those attacks never injured anyone when Ms. Kennedy was there, though one shell did hit close enough to rattle the Education Center. Further, she endured a more threatening mortar attack while administering tests at Kandahar.

Pamela's comments today show, yet again, the core proficiency always operating at Central Texas College: "We had a special relationship with service members. We were there to support them directly, and they knew it, so they treated us with a lot of respect. We worked twelve hours a day, seven days a week. Whatever it took to provide support, as long as we followed established policies, we did it."

" OUR REACH IS TREMENDOUS, AND YET IT'S DIFFERENT EVERYWHERE. WE CUSTOMIZE OUR CURRICULUM AND OUR PROGRAM FOR EVERY SITUATION. "
—JAN ANDERSON

A host of other adaptations in the last twenty years show CTC's continuing ability to do whatever it takes to be effective:

- For years, CTC could not teach classes on Fort Bragg (North Carolina) but did at nearby Pope Air Force Base. However, at the Pope graduations, Bill Beebe notes, "the students would all be in green uniforms, because they'd come over from Bragg to take our courses. It got almost embarrassing to be at a graduation at an Air Force base and there were two airmen and a hundred GIs."

Jim Yeonopolus (right), interim chancellor, enjoys a moment "in uniform" with a soldier enroute to a deployed area to meet with CTC staff.

- During the first Gulf War, enrollments on Central Campus and Fort Hood plummeted, and local businesses suffered. Mr. Beebe says, "That's when we became more proactive with military families. By the next Gulf War, we didn't have the same exodus, because CTC, and especially the Killeen Chamber of Commerce, accommodated the families to keep them here."

- In 1993, CTC offered courses on seventy-four Pacific Fleet and seventy-two Atlantic Fleet Ships.

Among CTC's first contracts was one with the Navy. In addition to serving students at sea, CTC has offered classroom courses through Navy College offices around the globe.

- In 1994, the school served more than 60,000 students, had more than 150,000 enrollments, and taught at 206 sites worldwide.

- In 1995, the college completed its 52,000-square-foot Nursing and Science Building. In 1999, it initiated construction for a 56,000-square-foot sports facility, a 16,000-square-foot library addition, an 8,300-square-foot aviation hangar, and a 55,000-square-foot Planetarium and Education Technology Center.

A unique way of celebrating a graduation—on the deck of an aircraft carrier. Dr. Anderson, then chancellor, is to the far left in this Photo.

- In 1995, Fort Polk took six classes to Haiti during troop deployments, and Leslie Whitman of the Navy Campus received a Navy Achievement Medal for "single-handedly" developing "the most comprehensive and successful shipboard educational program in the U.S. Navy," according to the citation.

- In 1995, new college programs opened simultaneously at four locations in Panama and one in Honduras. Enrollments more than doubled predictions.

- In 1996, instructors from the European campus followed deployments to Bosnia and Hungary, set up in squad tents with a field table and chair, and taught day and night to accommodate soldiers' twelve-hour shifts.

- In 1996, Fort Leonard Wood offered twelve associate degree programs, four times as many as when it opened.

- In 1996, the flight team was named the top two-year school in the national competition in Florida; that year and the next it won first place overall in the regional SAFECON competition.

The 1996 CTC national champion flight team.

The CTC Aviation Science program included flight training for helicopter and single engine planes.

- Under the direction of Ulla Torres, the Fort Lewis (Washington) site became renowned for its foreign language program. In 1996, the Army recognized 201st Military Intelligence Brigade there as the "best command language program of 1996 in the entire US Army."

- In 1997, the Navy Pacific Office in San Diego placed nine instructors on six ships headed to six-month deployments in the Western Pacific. They taught thirty-seven classes in the first six weeks.

> " I HOPE THE COMMUNITY REALIZES WHAT A TREMENDOUS ASSET OUR COLLEGE IS, NOT JUST BECAUSE OF WHAT WE DO AS FAR AS OFFERING EDUCATIONAL SERVICES, BUT THE FACT THAT WE DO IT AT SUCH A GREAT VALUE TO THE TAXPAYER. "
>
> —MARGARET BAY, FORMER PRESIDENT OF BOARD OF TRUSTEES

CTC'S FACULTY

This work has focused primarily on the college's leadership, which initiated a growth that is perhaps unique in American community colleges. However, as those leaders repeatedly acknowledge, none of it would have been possible—nor would the school have weathered the crisis of the late 1980s—without a faculty that continuously delivers on the administrators' grand promises.

It is difficult to depict teaching in a compelling way, because, despite the Hollywood portrayal of the eccentric instructor—Robin Williams standing on a chair in Dead Poets Society and shouting "Oh Captain! My Captain"—teaching is a paradox of grind: it is a repetitive process that must be made fresh for students receiving the material for the first time.

In many ways, CTC professors are like those at any other college. Class after class, semester after semester, they teach sentence fragments, plate tectonics, federalism, molecular metabolism, and the Battle of Bunker Hill. They guard against plagiarism, differentiate between lame and legitimate excuses, and promote evaluation over memorization.

At the same time, certain features of CTC faculty seem specific to the school, especially when considered in the aggregate. John Henderson, who taught English for forty-some years at the college, notes, "We have always been proud that we kept the standards high. We were sympathetic but also hard-nosed." His colleague Dennis Williams taught for just as long, and reveals what he brought to the classroom when he talks about the imagined difference between college and "real life." He says, "College is real life. You have to be punctual and prepared, you have to stay the full time, and you have to have relationships with your colleagues and your boss. College is about how you relate to the world."

John Henderson was an engaging English professor who began his teaching career at CTC in 1970. In 2003, Henderson would be named chairperson of the Communications Department.

CTC professors remember fondly their work and their collegiality. Ken Word's first set of office supplies included, in total, a box of rubber bands, a box of staples, a stapler, and a tape dispenser. He recalls being a math professor who shared office space with Williams and Henderson: "I was stuck between two English teachers for five years. It was brutal." Perhaps because they had Dr. Word cornered for so long, the two English professors spin this situation more positively: "Sharing office space with other departments was always stimulating."

Dr. Farnad J. Darnell, sociology professor, indicates just how atypical teaching at CTC could be:

One of my fondest memories was teaching at sea in 2007. There is nothing comparable to an aircraft carrier landing. My thoughts focused on how young these soldiers and sailors were, and what their backstories were.

Their opinions on current issues were very diverse and broad. I loved the insight and the knowledge I gained from them.

And I had an opportunity to teach at Walter Reed Naval Hospital in Bethesda, Maryland. This seemed like a logical chronology—from ship to shore. In one class I had two men wounded from fights in Afghanistan. Again, I learned so much from the students.

I would not trade this experience for anything in the world.

CTC's Central Campus is home to a large number of international students. Jan Anderson, current dean of Central Campus, has fond memories of her time as an English as a second language instructor.

An unusually cooperative relationship between faculty and administration is another distinctive feature of the college. Echoing statements from others, John Henderson says, "I thought I would teach at CTC two or three years and move on to something bigger and better. But I liked it so much that I stayed forty years. I loved teaching, and the administration let us do our job."

> They always step up.
> And they would do that
> whether I was here or not.
> —DEAN JANICE ANDERSON,
> ON THE CTC FACULTY

Dennis Williams agrees. "Most of us stayed at Central Texas College because the administration let us teach our classes the way we knew they should be taught." He adds, "Anywhere you go there is a tension between the administration and the faculty. Ours was a healthy tension."

Administrators concur with this assessment. Chancellor Anderson states simply, "I never felt like I was at war with the faculty." Jan Anderson, dean of Central and Service Area Campus, adds:

At forums I hear about faculty fighting with their administration. I hear about some ugly things, and I'm so glad that's not us.

The faculty here has faced almost overwhelming challenges, especially in the last year, because of changes in the military and other changes. But they always step up. And they would do that whether I was here or not. They are remarkable.

Jan recounts another occurrence that, as much as any single episode, captures the remarkable relationship among students, faculty, and administration. When the dorms closed during winter break of 2001, international students needed somewhere to stay. Only three months had passed since the terrorist attacks in New York and Washington, and in this potentially unfriendly atmosphere, Ms. Anderson, at that time in the ESL Department, simply invited a dozen or so to stay at her house.

She never asked them to, but they cooked dinner every night—an international smorgasbord and also a fine example of instant karma for Jan. They watched TV late at night but stayed as quiet as church mice when she went to bed.

One morning, as she tiptoed around their makeshift bedding arrayed across her living room floor, she noticed shopping bags attached to everyone's head. She later learned they had all dyed their hair the night before, and the bags prevented the coloring from rubbing off on her linens.

What college could tell a comparable tale?

A CTC SUCCESS STORY

Abdul Subhani came from Pakistan to Texas in 2000. A young, ambitious man, Abdul left Hillsboro for Killeen and remembers to this day the remarkably friendly assistance he received from Cynthia Burrus, his very first contact at the school.

> It is CTC's employees, and not just its delivery systems, that offer accessibility.

Abdul planned on finishing his general education and heading to UT, "but I loved it here and stayed." He became vice president for the International Students Association, and along the way "I bugged Dr. Anderson a lot to not raise tuition. And he surely did not the two years I was there."

He completed his degree in 2002 and began accumulating IT certifications. He also worked for Dr. John Frith in the Business Administration lab, and Dr. Frith, along with Les Ledger, began mentoring Abdul. In fact, after 9/11, Adbul called Professor Ledger "after midnight more than once" with various concerns. Mr. Subhani next worked with Teresa Chavez in Continuing Education to develop computer courses for senior citizens, and then HR hired him to teach Microsoft Outlook to employees.

After finishing his bachelor's degree, Abdul began graduate school at Tarleton State (formerly ATU) and worked for the Killeen Boys and Girls Clubs. Altogether, then, he had four jobs at once, and yet he also managed to write grant proposals that brought in $170,000 of computer equipment to the Clubs. As a result he was promoted to a position sufficient to earn his work (H-1) visa. He finished his master's degree and promptly received a job offer in Dallas. Local entrepreneur Wallace Vernon shredded that offer and hired Abdul at Medical Office Management. In 2006 the two men opened Centex Technologies.

Alumni Abdul Subhani, a local entrepreneur, got his start at Central Texas College.

About that same time, Abdul contacted Deputy Chancellor Bill Alexander about teaching in the Computer Science Department. The two men often chatted when Abdul worked in the Business Department lab. Today, Abdul still teaches as an adjunct for Department Chair Katherine Oser.

Mr. Subhani serves on the CTC Foundation Board, chairs the Computer Science Department Advisory Committee, and maintains the Subhani Scholarship Foundation. He became a U.S. citizen in April 2014. He remarks that in addition to those already mentioned, Barbara Merlo and Jan Anderson also "helped me very much."

Abdul's experience perfectly demonstrates the components that produce CTC's continuing success. In his initial contact with the school, a staff member made him feel welcome. The faculty identified and guided an ambitious, capable student, and administrators all the way up to the chancellor made themselves available to him. In other words, it is CTC's employees, and not just its delivery systems, that offer accessibility. And finally, local business leaders followed through on the college's good work, doing what it took to keep Abdul here.

This is no Cinderella story, as the press dubbed CTC's very first enrollment. Instead, the service and professionalism of people throughout the college and Killeen ensured that one man's talent and hard work allowed him to live the American Dream.

Students of the real world—no matter where in the world they may be—have always found that same opportunity at Central Texas College.

Dr. Jim Anderson, CTC chancellor, retired in 2012 after more than twenty years of service to the college.

> *"Our competitor schools charge three, four, five times as much. I ask them, 'What is it you provide that I don't?' And the answer is nothing. I don't agree that we should just get as much as we can from the students."*

—JIM YEONOPOLUS

Remarkably, two chancellors have served Central Texas College for 90 percent of its fifty-year existence. Dr. Anderson replaced a man who many regarded with awe. However, the school's crisis somewhat balanced this unenviable position. There was virtually nowhere to go but up.

Dr. Thomas Klincar, appointed chancellor in February 2012, served twenty-eight years in the United States Air Force (USAF) and retired as a full colonel. He worked in high-level administrative positions for the College for Enlisted Professional Military Education (USAF), the Community College of the Air Force, and the NATO School. A former English professor and vocational/technical instructor, he earned a doctor of arts from De La Salle University, and before coming to CTC he served as president of John Wood Community College in Illinois.[1]

In a recent oral history interview, when asked for biographical background on how he came to be here, the "new" chancellor manages to talk about himself for a couple minutes but soon veers into a discourse about his longstanding admiration for Central Texas College: "We absolutely excel at providing the same quality of education in far off locations that a student receives on Central Campus. There is still no college that can do many of the things we do."

The first college course Dr. Klincar's wife Deborah attended was at a CTC site in Florida; as an Air Force officer, Dr. Klincar saw CTC sites all over the world; and he had known Dr. Anderson for many years and often sought his advice. The chancellor states that "having the chance to come to an institution that I had known for three decades, that my family was a part of, and whose previous chancellor was a mentor of mine—it was a blessing."

◀ CTC graduations are held around the world. Recent Europe graduates are pictured in this photo.

1. Dr. Thomas Klincar resigned as this book was going to press. Although the next chapter in the CTC history will be written by a new leader, Dr. Klincar was able to realize many important goals during his tenure.

Just as the Greiner Curve helps explain the transition at Central Texas College in the late 1980s, it provides context for the transition to this administration. In a "growth through alliances" stage, organizations often use strategies like outsourcing and partnerships, and while CTC has always partnered, numerous recent initiatives clearly indicate this style of growth:

Left to right: Specialist Jesse Alguire, Specialist Rain Forest Stone, and Sergeant Jeremiah Pike discuss the software program they designed for the Microsoft-CTC Cohort 4 class project.

- A technology partnership among Central Texas College, Fort Hood, and Microsoft provides that the company will fly any student completing the certification to Washington for a job interview.

- The college develops a curriculum with the city of Marble Falls to help staff a new Scott and White hospital. CTC not only sends nurses there but also develops career pathways and education for entry-level jobs.

- The Hill Country University Center Foundation, Central Texas College, Austin Community College, and Texas Tech have collaborated to offer CTC classes in Fredericksburg that will transfer seamlessly to the four-year university.

- CTC collaborates with the Bell County Sheriff's Department in establishing an area law enforcement academy.

- With the Killeen Independent School District, CTC is initiating an Early College High School program for first-generation college students.

- CTC partners with twenty-seven schools to provide dual credit high school/college classes and with Texas A&M/Central Texas in a "2-plus-2" program. Both initiatives, begun under Chancellor Anderson, greatly reduce the cost of a college education.

- Continuing its partnership—in the broadest and best sense—with the U.S. military, CTC allowed soldiers who lost their tuition assistance during the Congressional impasse of 2013 to attend school for free. All together, the college waived about $1 million.

> **CTC IS MORE THAN JUST A COLLEGE CAMPUS TO ME. IT IS THE PLACE WHERE I HAVE TRANSITIONED FROM A YOUNG GIRL TO A CAREER-AND GOAL-ORIENTED YOUNG WOMAN WHO IS FULLY PREPARED FOR MY NEXT TRANSITION IN LIFE. IT IS BECAUSE OF THE HELP FROM MY CTC FAMILY THAT I HAVE BEEN ABLE TO ACCOMPLISH ALL THAT I HAVE.**
> —BIANCA NICOLE PATRICE NICKLEBERRY

Meanwhile, CTC faces a host of new challenges. Chancellor Klincar notes, "We can transport pallets of textbooks and marry them up with a ship in an African port or in a war zone." However, as he notes, these logistical proficiencies provide less of a competitive edge in an age of electronic curricula.

In addition, a challenge for Central Campus, as on all college campuses today, involves facilities and amenities. Students familiar with interactive tabletop displays and tablet syncing on the one hand, and suite-style dorms and luxury lounges on the other, often decide which college to attend based largely on such expectations. Dr. Klincar asserts, "To be competitive, we need to have the same level of facilities as other educational institutions in our area."

When he discusses these matters, the chancellor's words are interchangeable with those from people who drove CTC's successes in the past: "We need to create and deliver learning environments wherever our students are in the fashion in which they want to learn."

Other complications confront the college, as both Chancellor Klincar and General Rex Weaver, the chair of the Board of Trustees, have recently noted. These include the government sequestration, constraints on education from the military, and an unprecedented regulation of higher education. The latest reauthorization of the Higher Education Act requires a state license to operate on federal military installations, whose own regulations, in turn, differ from the state in which they reside. And each state has different regulations. The daunting magnitude of such Orwellian stipulations dovetails with the Texas Success Initiative and the federal Student Success Program, which apply a model based on traditional four-year students to measure college success everywhere. The one-size-fits-all approach misses the circumstances of community college students, especially those subject to the demands of serving in our military.

CTC reinstated its Police Academy program in 2014. Graduates of that first Basic Peace Officer class were Cadets Warren Scott II, Manuel Pedroza, Jennifer Amezquita, Marisol Barron, Bryan Mahan, and John Lake.

> # "WE'RE LIKE THE OLD BRITISH EMPIRE— THE SUN NEVER SETS ON CTC.
> —GENERAL REX WEAVER

Regardless of these challenges, both the past and continuing success of CTC derive from a paradox: the college thrives by doing what it has always done, but doing what it has always done means always changing. Bill Beebe acknowledges this when he says, "Our ability to adjust to the marketplace rapidly has been the key to our successes." While this is true of most private-sector organizations, the college has always done it at least as well as any institution of higher learning. Rapid adjustment occurred with Dr. Morton planting CTC flags around the globe, and it occurred with API, with Dr. Anderson's targeted growth, and with distance education, to name a few.

At the same time, two unchanging institutional traits have woven their way through the school's history. For one, it has always led the community college emphasis on a student-centered education, tailored to the needs of the people it serves. Its innovations have repeatedly become the norm.

CTC is number one with 2013 Fort Riley graduate Ryan Sweesy, a member of the "Big Red One."

The second, related trait is an ability to accomplish the task, regardless of any obstacles. Whether they squat in pickup beds in South Korea, wrestle prehistoric copying machines in the Philippines, dine on canned meat in Iraq and sweat through food poisoning in Maryland, offer opportunity to the dispossessed in Gatesville, discuss John Quincy Adams in Quonset huts, or don body armor at forward operating bases in Afghanistan, the people of Central Texas College continuously practice the principle expressed best by Jim Yeonopolus: "If someone tells me it can't be done, that really gets to me. I don't believe that at all, about anything."

Sailors aboard the USS *Ingraham* take advantage of CTC's Naval Afloat program and are able to take classes while at sea.

BIBLIOGRAPHY

American Association of Community Colleges: http://www.aacc.nche.edu/AboutCC/history/Pages/pasttopresent.aspx

Anonymous, "A History of Central Texas College." Ca. 1990.

Bell County Historical Commission. *Story of Bell County, Texas*. Eakin Press, 1988.

Blodgett, Terrell. "Management Study of the American Educational Complex College District, Killeen, TX." Lyndon B. Johnson School of Public Affairs, University of Texas at Austin, 1989.

Central Texas College, Catalogue Archives. http://www.ctcd.edu/academics/catalog/catalog-archives/

Central Texas College, *The CTCD Communicator*. Nine issues, Summer 1994–Fall 1999.

Central Texas College, "40 Years." (Pamphlet from 40th anniversary celebration), 2005.

Central Texas College memo, "Central Texas College District: Duties and Responsibilities." September 1994.

Faulk, Odie B. and Laura E. *Fort Hood: The First 50 Years*. Frank W. Mayborn Foundation, 1990.

Greiner, Larry E. "Evolution and Revolution as Organizations Grow." *Harvard Business Review*, Volume 50 (4), 1972.

Johnson, Lyndon D. "Remarks at the Dedication of Central Texas College, Killeen, Texas," December 12, 1967. Online by Gerhard Peters and John T. Woolley, *The American Presidency Project*. http://www.presidency.ucsb.edu/ws/?pid=28597.

    See also, http://www.youtube.com/watch?v=v9MEjwfNj8w

Killeen Daily Herald. "American Educational Complex 10th Anniversary Edition." September 11, 1977.

Manfull, Dan. "Background Information about the History of Central Texas College." Unpublished paper, n.d.

Morton, Luis Jac-Remelg. "Central Texas College: Concept to Decennial." Doctoral dissertation, East Texas State University, December 1992.

Sisson, James R. "A Historical Review of the Governance and Administration of a Global Community College." Doctoral dissertation, Baylor University, December 2005.

Sisson, Phyllis Ann Paul. "A Case Study of a Faculty's Perception of the Decision Making Processes in a Texas Community College." Doctoral dissertation, Baylor, December 1997.

Skidmore, Gerald D., Sr. *Historic Killeen*. Historical Publishing Network, 2010.

Smyrl, Vivian Elizabeth. "Coryell County," *Handbook of Texas Online* (http://www.tshaonline.org/handbook/online/articles/hcc23).

Summers, Barbara Stodghil. "Military Student Attitudes Toward American Preparatory Institute and Competency-Based, Continuous-Progress Instruction." MA Thesis, ATU, 1975. http://files.eric.ed.gov/fulltext/ED118901.pdf

Texas A&M University Central Texas. "5-Year Strategic Plan: 2011–2015." http://www.tamuct.edu/departments/president/extras/TAMUCTSP11-15Final.pdf

Walker, Kenneth. "Project Transition and Junior College Response: Study of an Innovation." Doctoral dissertation, University of Texas at Austin, 1973.

Witt, A., J. Wattenbarger, J. Collattscheck, and J. Suppiger. *America's Community Colleges: The First Century*. Washington, DC: Community College Press, 1994.

ORAL HISTORY INTERVIEWS
(ALL INTERVIEWS IN PERSON UNLESS OTHERWISE NOTED)

Alexander, Bill. July 29, 2014.

Anderson, James. July 3, 2014.

Anderson, Janice. October 3, 2014.

Beebe, Bill. November 6, 2014.

Chapman, Suzi. August 7, 2014.

Farris, Ann. August 29, 2014.

Hull, Monica. August 29, 2014.

Henderson, John and Dennis Williams. July 30, 2014.

Isdale, Scott. December 16, 2014.

Kennedy, Pamela. January 13, 2015.

Kliewer, Mary. July 22, 2014.

Klincar, Thomas. January 8, 2015.

Meyer, Mari. December 9, 2014.

Nixon, James. July 10, 2014.

Roach, William A. August 11, 2014 (phone interview).

Rudolph, Max. July 10, 2014.

Rummel, Gus. January 14, 2015 (phone interview).

Subhani, Abdul. September 5, 2014.

Swartz, Phillip. December 8, 2014.

Waldrop, Joan. July 16, 2014 (phone interview).

Walker, Kenneth. September 21, 2014 (phone interview).

Weaver, General Rex and Barbara. October 17, 2014.

Welsh, Johnelle. July 14, 2014.

Word, Kenneth. August 12, 2014.

Yeonopolus, Jim. July 3, 2014.

Yeilding, David and Donnie. January 7, 2015.

BOARD MEMBERS

CENTRAL TEXAS COLLEGE
COLLEGE

The Central Texas College Board of Trustees is comprised of elected representatives from the College District. Trustees serve six-year at-large terms representing the District, which includes the Killeen and Copperas Cove Independent School Districts.

CENTRAL TEXAS COLLEGE DISTRICT BOARD OF TRUSTEES, 2015

Seated, left to right: Reverend Jimmy Towers, vice chair; Mrs. Mari Meyer, chair; and Brigadier General Charles Rex Weaver, treasurer.
Standing, left to right: Dr. Scott Isdale, secretary; Mr. Bill Beebe; Mr. Jim Yeonopolus, interim chancellor; Mr. Elwood "Woody" Shemwell; and Mr. Don Armstrong.

CHAIRS
BOARD OF TRUSTEES

Mr. William Bigham, July 1965–April 1979

Dr. William Roach, April 1979–May 1989

Mr. Riley Simpson, May 1989–January 1997

Mrs. Margaret Bay, May 1997–May 1999

Charles Baggett, May 1999–

Mrs. Mari Meyer, May 2009–May 2013

Brigadier General (Ret.-TX) Charles Rex Weaver, May 2013–May 2015

Mrs. Mari Meyer, May 2015–Present

CENTRAL TEXAS COLLEGE DISTRICT
ORIGINAL BOARD OF TRUSTEES

Seated, left to right: Marvin Mickan; Guinn Fergus; Mrs. Linus Frederick, secretary; and J. A. Darossett.
Standing, left to right: Birt F. Wilkerson, vice president; Mr. William Bigham, president; Dr. Luis Morton, chancellor; and Dr. W. A. Roach, treasurer.